AF348703

Water Forgets Its Own Name

Water Forgets Its Own Name

Jude Neale

&

Nicholas Jennings

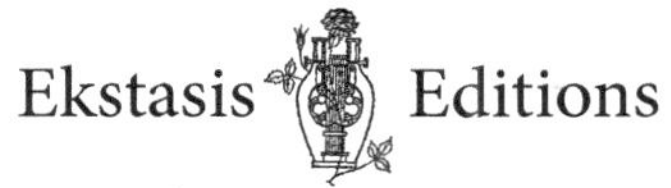

Ekstasis Editions

Poems Copyright @ Jude Neale, 2023
Cover Art: Snowy Sunset at Bowen Bay, watercolour
Copyright @ Nick Jennings, 2003
Interior Art @ Nick Jennings

Published in 2023 by:
Ekstasis Editions Canada Ltd., Box 8474, Main Postal Outlet, Victoria, B.C. V8W 3S1

All rights reserved. No part of this book may be reproduced in any form without the written permission of the publisher, with the exception of brief passages in reviews. Any request for pho-tocopying or other reproduction of any part of this book should be directed in writing to the publisher or to ACCESS: The Ca-nadian Copyright Licensing Agency, One Yonge Street, Suite 800, Toronto, Ontario, Canada, M5E 1E5.

Library and Archives Canada Cataloguing in Publication

Title: Water forgets its own name / Jude Neale & Nicholas Jennings.
Names: Neale, Jude, author. | Jennings, Nicholas (Painter), illustrator.
Description: Poems by Jude Neale; paintings by Nicholas Jennings
Identifiers: Canadiana 20230489427 | ISBN 9781771715317 (hardcover) |
ISBN 9781771715300 (softcover)
Classification: LCC PS8627.E22 W38 2023 | DDC C811/.6—dc23

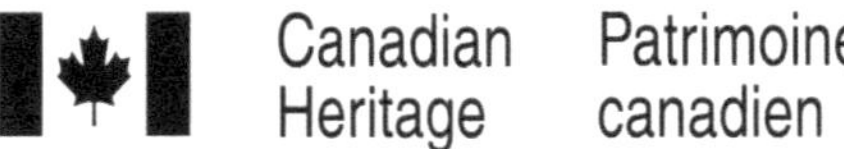

Ekstasis Editions acknowledges financial support for the publication of *Water Forgets Its Own Name* from the government of Canada through the Canada Book Fund, and from the Province of British Co-lumbia through the Book Publishing Tax Credit.

Printed and bound in Canada.

"I am the lover of uncontained and immortal beauty."
~ Walt Whitman, Leaves of Grass.

This book is dedicated to my beautiful children.

~ Nicholas Jennings

To the natural beauty nestled within all of our world's islands,
and to my extraordinary children and grandchildren.

~ Jude Neale.

We write and paint on Nexwlélexwm (Bowen Island), unceded traditional land of the Skwxwú7mesh Nation, and acknowledge the island's first storytellers.

CONTENTS

This book, *Water Forgets Its Own Name*, captures my place in the world. It speaks of Bowen Island, a small paradise in British Columbia's Salish Sea. The poems are saturated with the light and colour of everyday miracles seen through Nicholas Jennings paintings and the strong memories I hold of a place that I have lived in for four decades. I hope that you'll enjoy the tour of the ordinary and sublime, pressed like flowers, between its pages.

~ Jude Neale

During the launch event for her book *The Flaw*, Jude Neale broached the genius idea that we collaborate on a book of her poetry set to my art. I was both flattered and blown away by this exciting concept. I immediately shared Jude's vision: a significant cultural artefact memorializing an island rich in treasures for the soul. When I first moved to Bowen, I was dealing with severe PTSD, and I had a lot of trauma to process and heal from. I quickly discovered that the paintings that I was driven to do for their therapeutic value resonated with, and helped me build ties with, the local community. By my second year of living on Bowen, my art had found its way onto the cover of the Bowen Pages phone book, and by the third year, I had my first solo show here. Between the poetry and the art, I feel there is much to savour between the covers of this book. With one exception, the art featured in this book is all centred\on Bowen Island: its beaches, docks, creeks, sunsets and winding roads. I love how Jude has interwoven these scenes with her own story, extracting nuances of profound meaning with her clever poetry that melts in the ear and soothes the heart.

~ Nicholas Jennings

Water Forgets Its Own Name

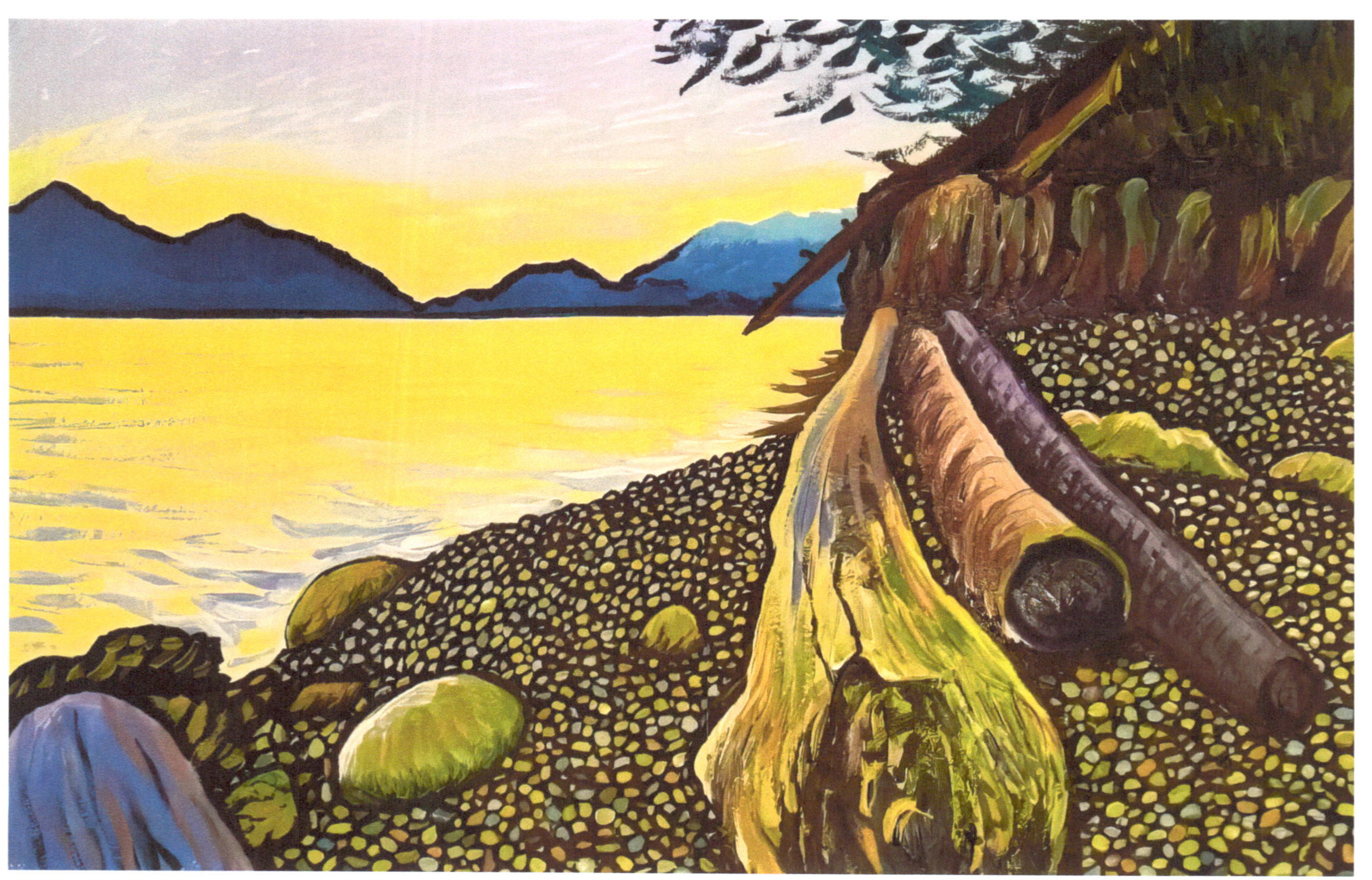

~ Crayola Beach, watercolour ~

PEBBLES AT DAWN

I sit on a sun washed log
Pressing the pebbles
Against my pale toes
What can you say
To the palette of yellow
That infuses my being
With the first morning light
In summer's warm promise
Of glorious sepia beginnings

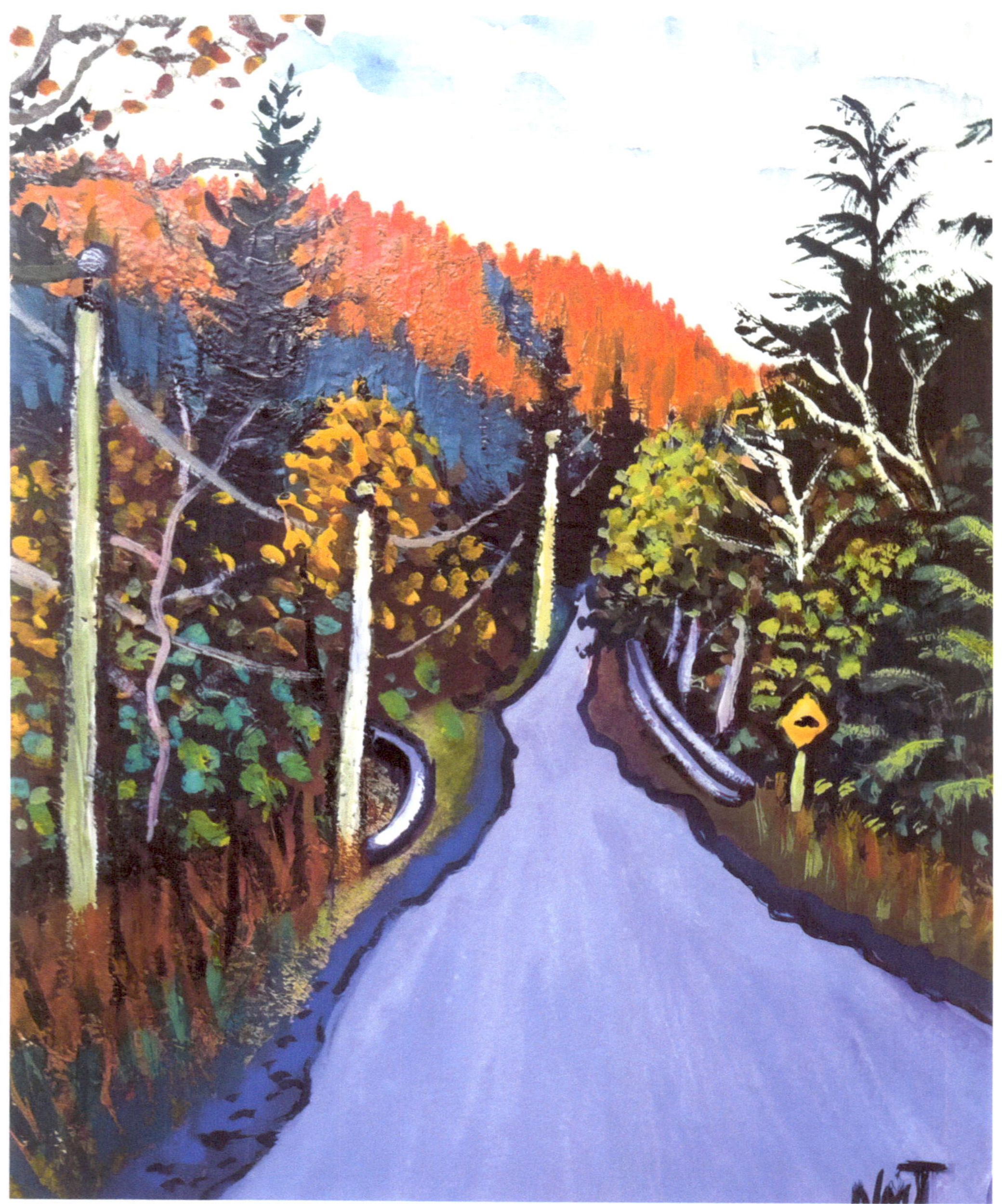

~ Sunrise on Mount Gardner, watercolour ~

Losing the dark,
a creep of sun,
on the backs
of late autumn
trees. They wave
their turning leaves
towards the light.
Transformation
happens here.
When the last
frog has spoken,
and the grass
is weary with
the weight
of dew.
All the world beckons,
to be unzipped,
made visible,
on this naked
September morn.

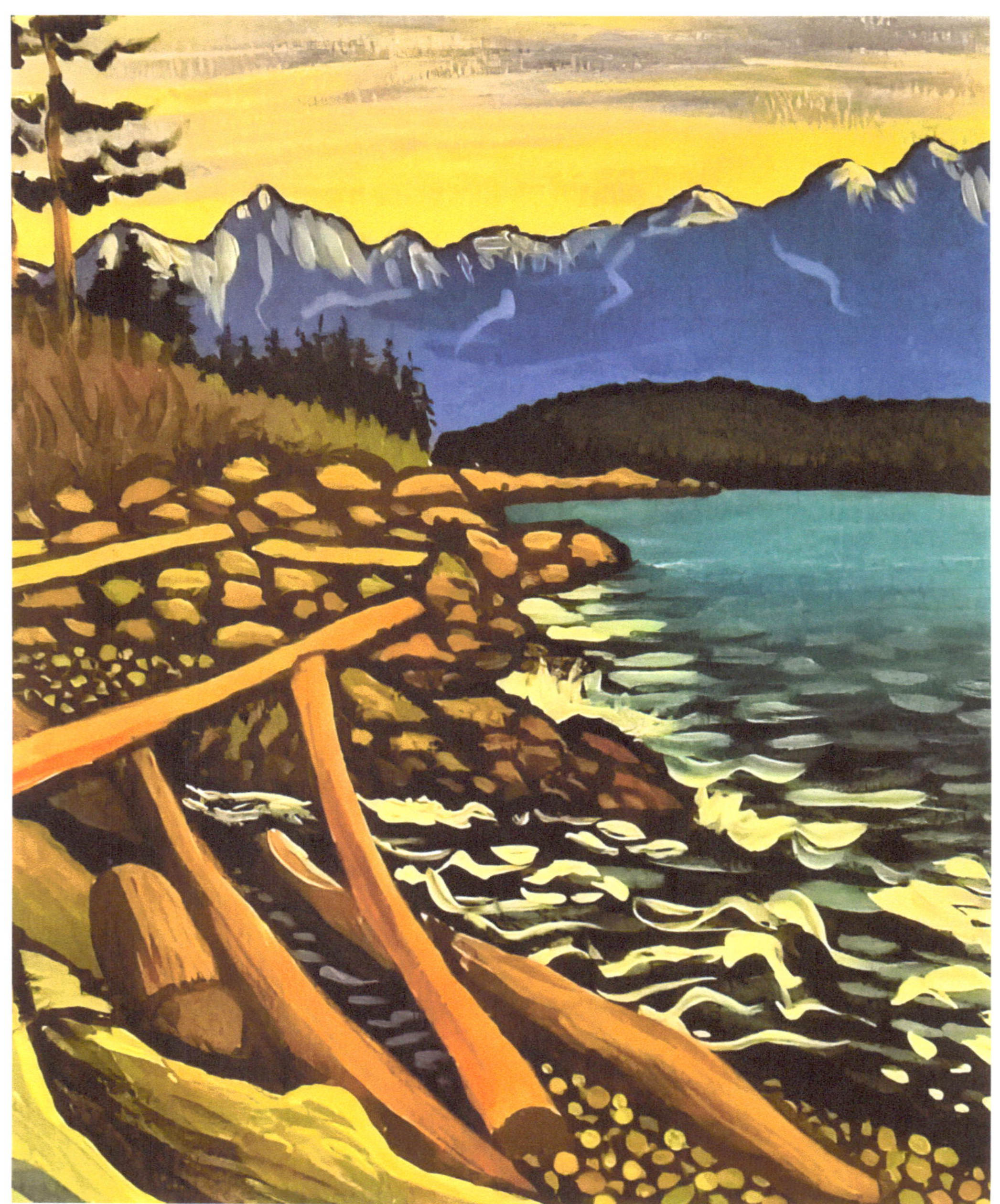

~ Cates Bay, watercolour ~

Caught in a Dream

One summer I swam alone
in the icy tongue of a fjord,
willing myself to breathe
in the glacial green
of Norway's waters.
Now, home, I paddle
up to my chest and float,
practical beach shoes
pointing to the North Star.
The glow of gold on blue
turns liquid turquoise.
Coastal Mountains behind,
frosted with the weight
of amber snow. I can feel
the suck of a waxing moon.
It brings me back—
to slick copper logs,
the sparkle of beach glass,
and the fortress of trees,
surrounding me,
like a Dream Catcher.

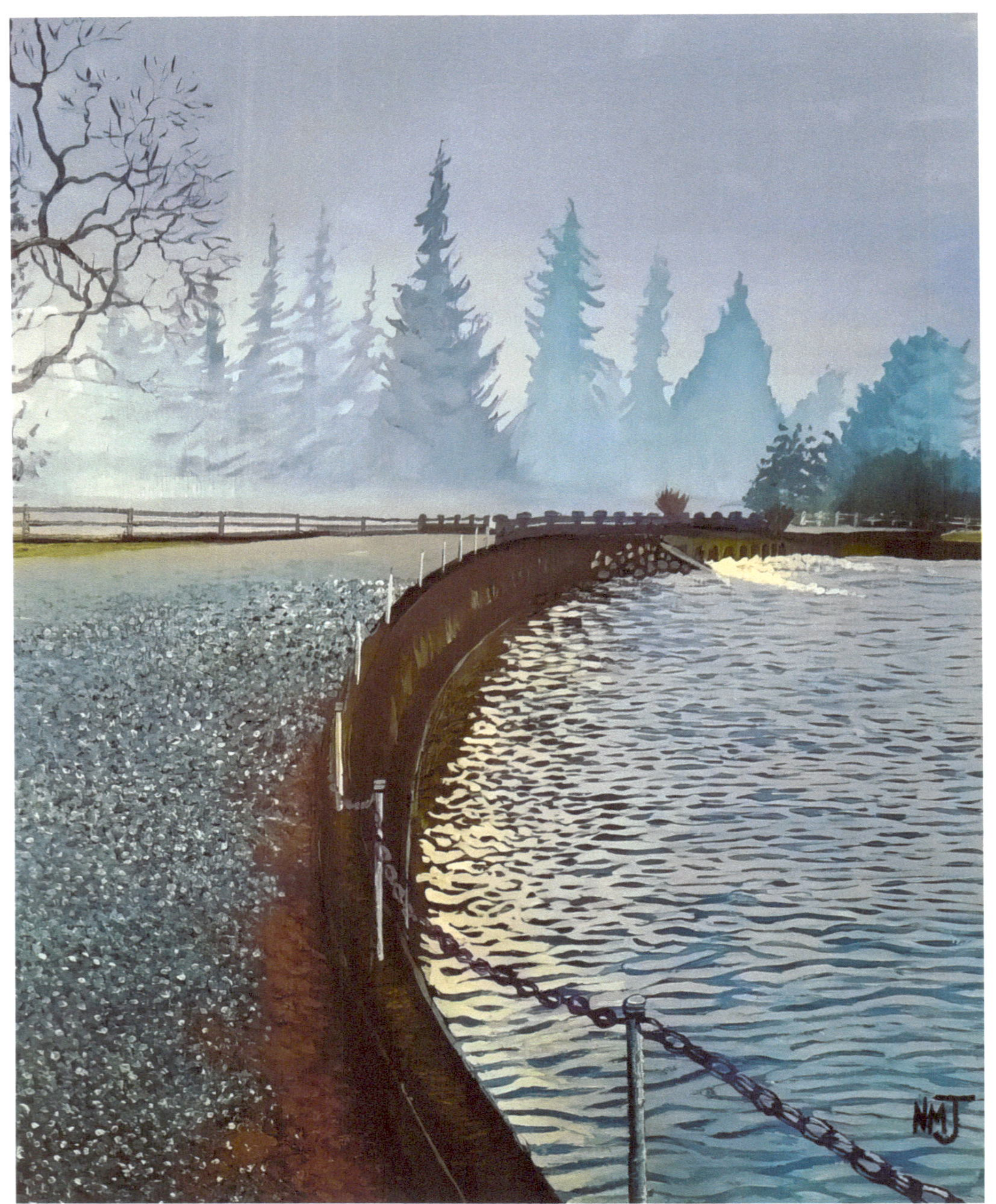

~ The Causeway, acrylic ~

Causeway in Fog

This is a place which aches
for the bloom of shimmer,
that's held in water—
still sleepy with the
weight of blue.
I want to penetrate this
scrim of snowy fog.
It settles quietly,
a white feather floating,
to the tops of the firs.
Let me graze the gilded fingers,
that stroke the bay's edge.
It leaves a sheen on the solitary path,
and wends gently between
the muted land and sea.
The sun's lustre fills me.
I'm a chalice, spilling over,
with the alchemy of gold.

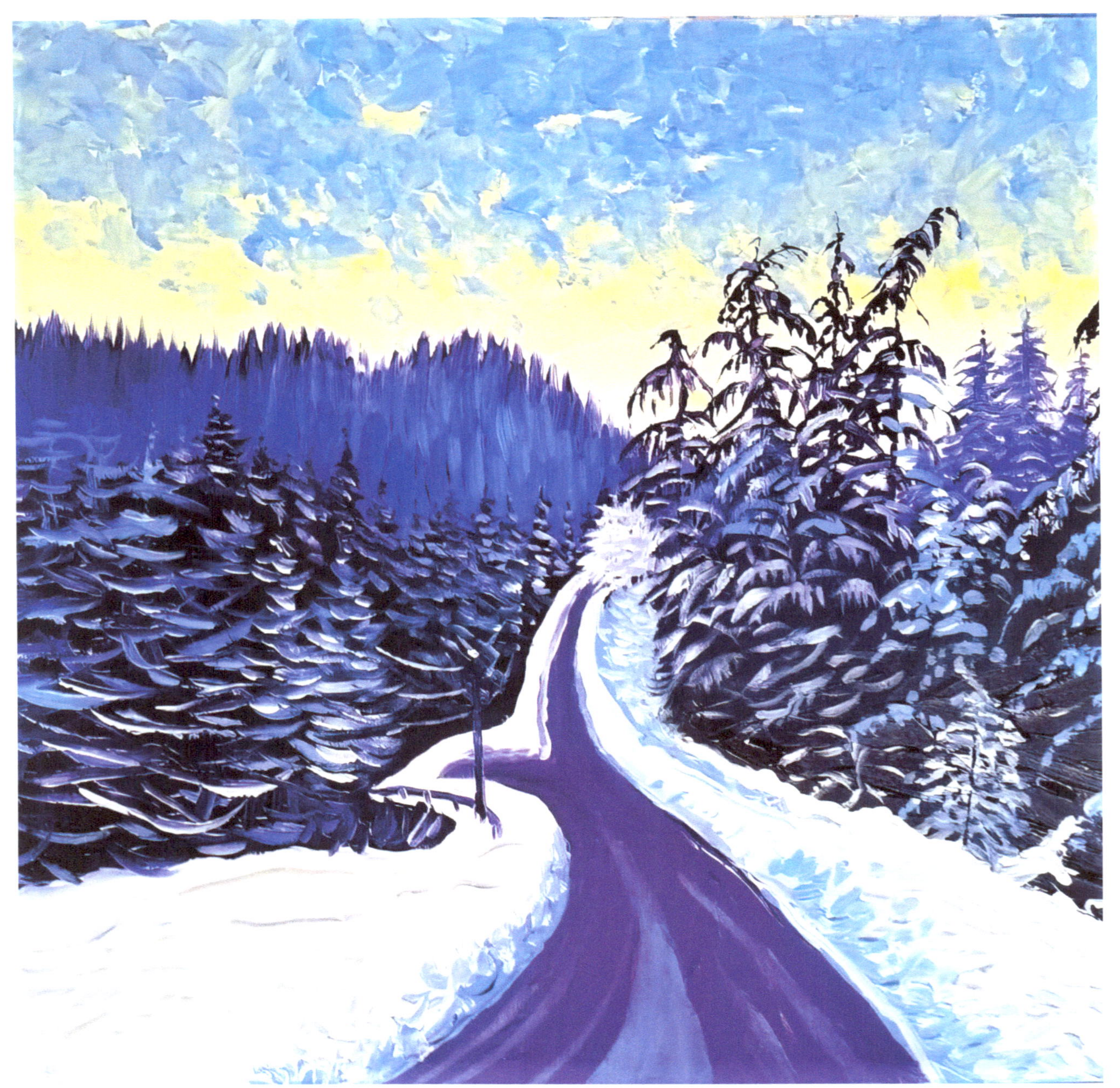

~ Buchanan Road, acrylic ~

Winter Crystal

The snow, a silk scarf,
wraps the world
in its cold beauty.
Roads are clear,
a blue ribbon slips
by the sheared verge.
Sentries of Christmas
trees are draped in lace.
And what do I know?
I know that there
is no other purpose
to living, than to become
part of it all, a blinding
reflection of light.

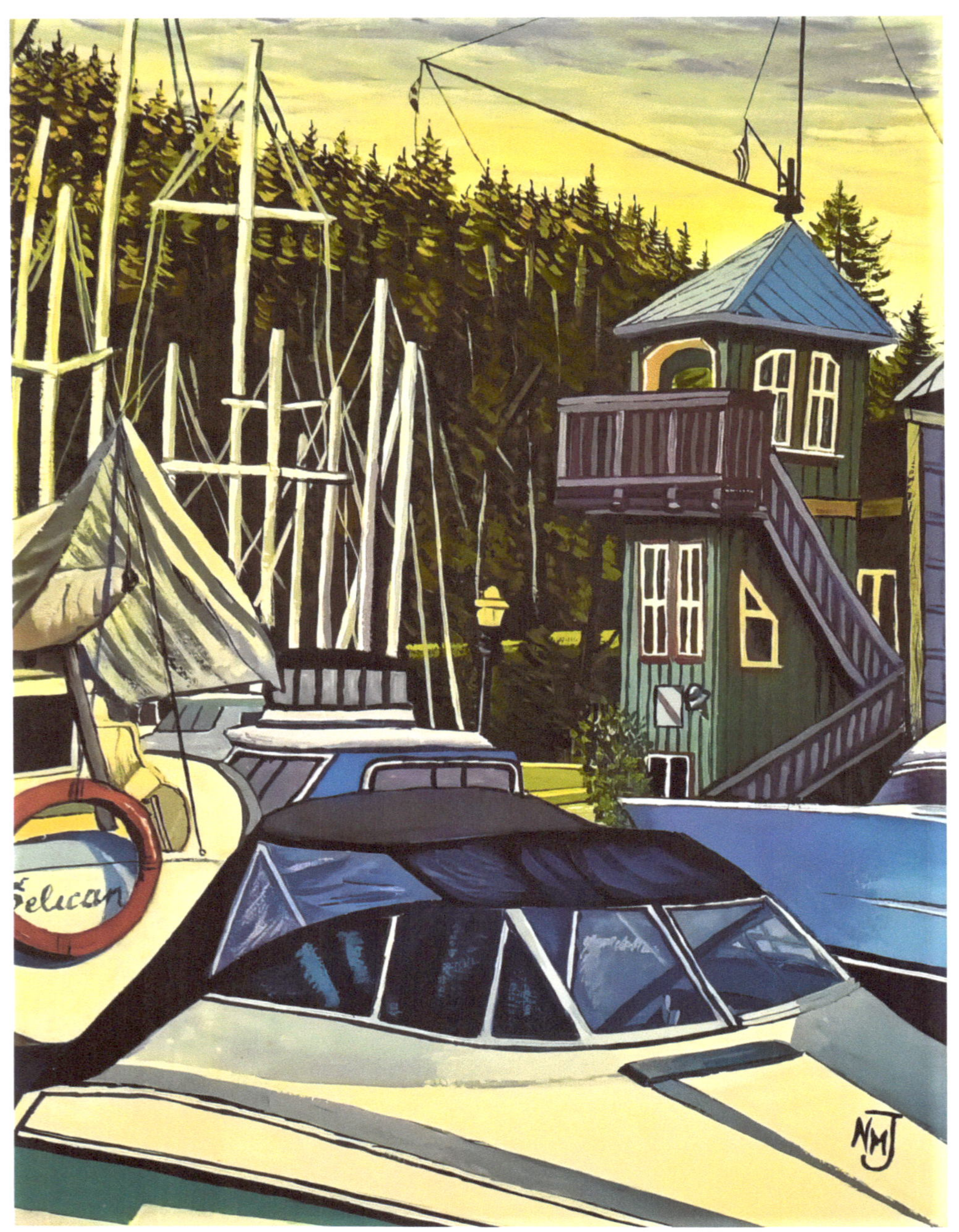

~ Union Steamship Company Marina, watercolour. ~

REMEMBRANCE DAY

On Remembrance Day
the community gathers
as one voice, to mark
the loved and forgotten.
Poppies fall like petals
onto the white cenotaph.
Voices sing of peace
and I don't know,
where I stand. Sometimes
I am caught in the sweetness
of the lone trumpeter,
playing taps from the top
of a tower.
How it draws us backwards
to muddy fields and marsh,
city streets and jungle. To
mourn death so far away,
yet still remembered. And yet
does this occasion marked
by 21-gun salutes,
and fly overs, stop
the deadly anger
that's spread between
scores of countries?
I don't want to celebrate
war, can't mouth the prayers,
or bow my head—not to forget, but to weep at the folly
dividing us, even as we beg,
for flowers to grow
in Flanders Field.

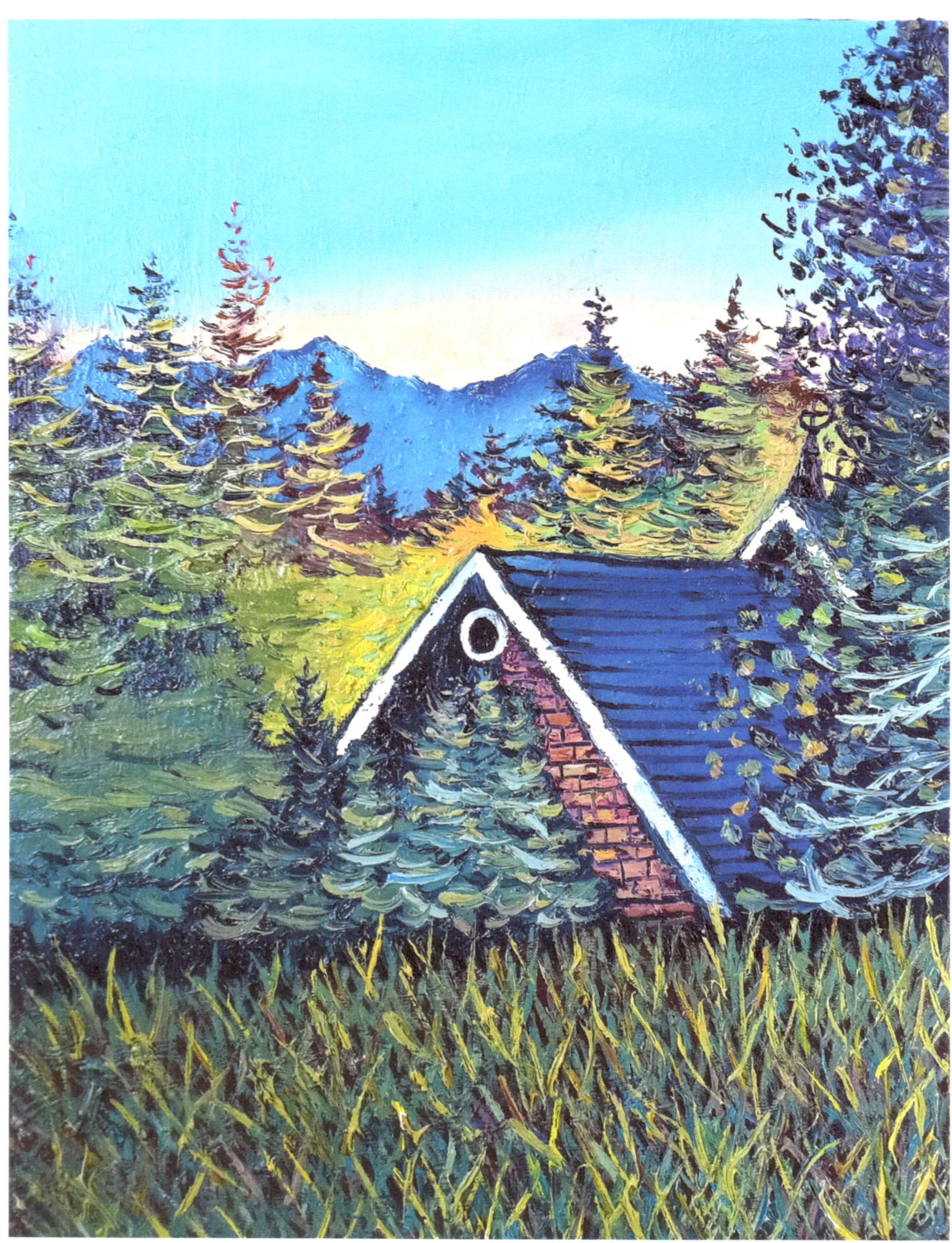

~ Cates Chapel, oil ~

Sunday Bells

The press of grass was
imprinted on my knees,
that time I listened to
the soft chorus
of children, painting
the chapel in pastels—
small voices
upturned in song.
My being warmed,
as I felt the words shine,
like a thousand small suns.
You are the world's
original innocence,
a bouquet of prayer flags,
scattering grace.
Your melody spreads
near and far, to places
of shadow, renewing
those hearts that are
tattered and torn.

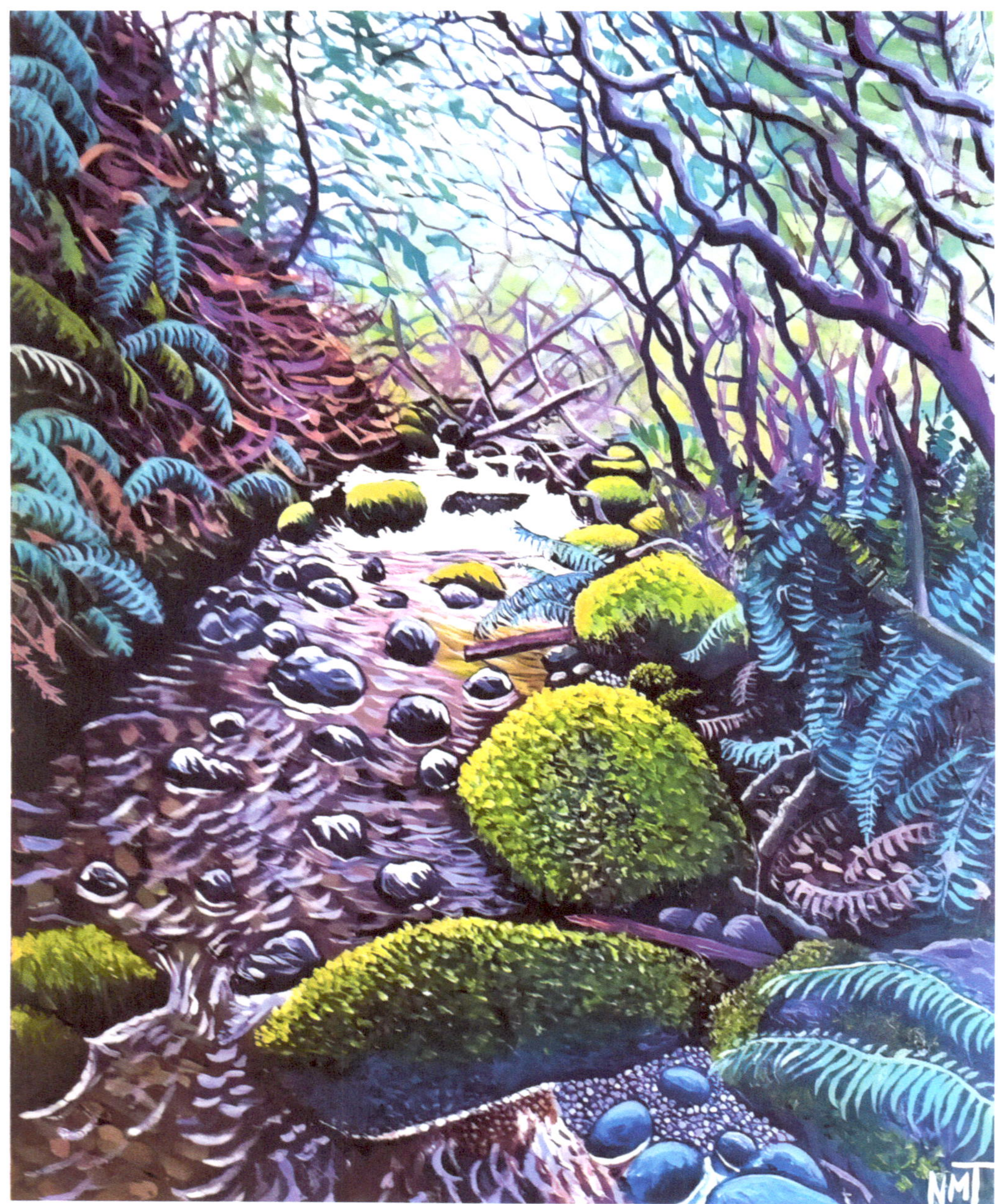

~ Creek on Mike's Lorg Trail, acrylic. ~

Water Forgets Its Own Name

in spring, a creek trickles
to a swollen lake—
water forgets its own name

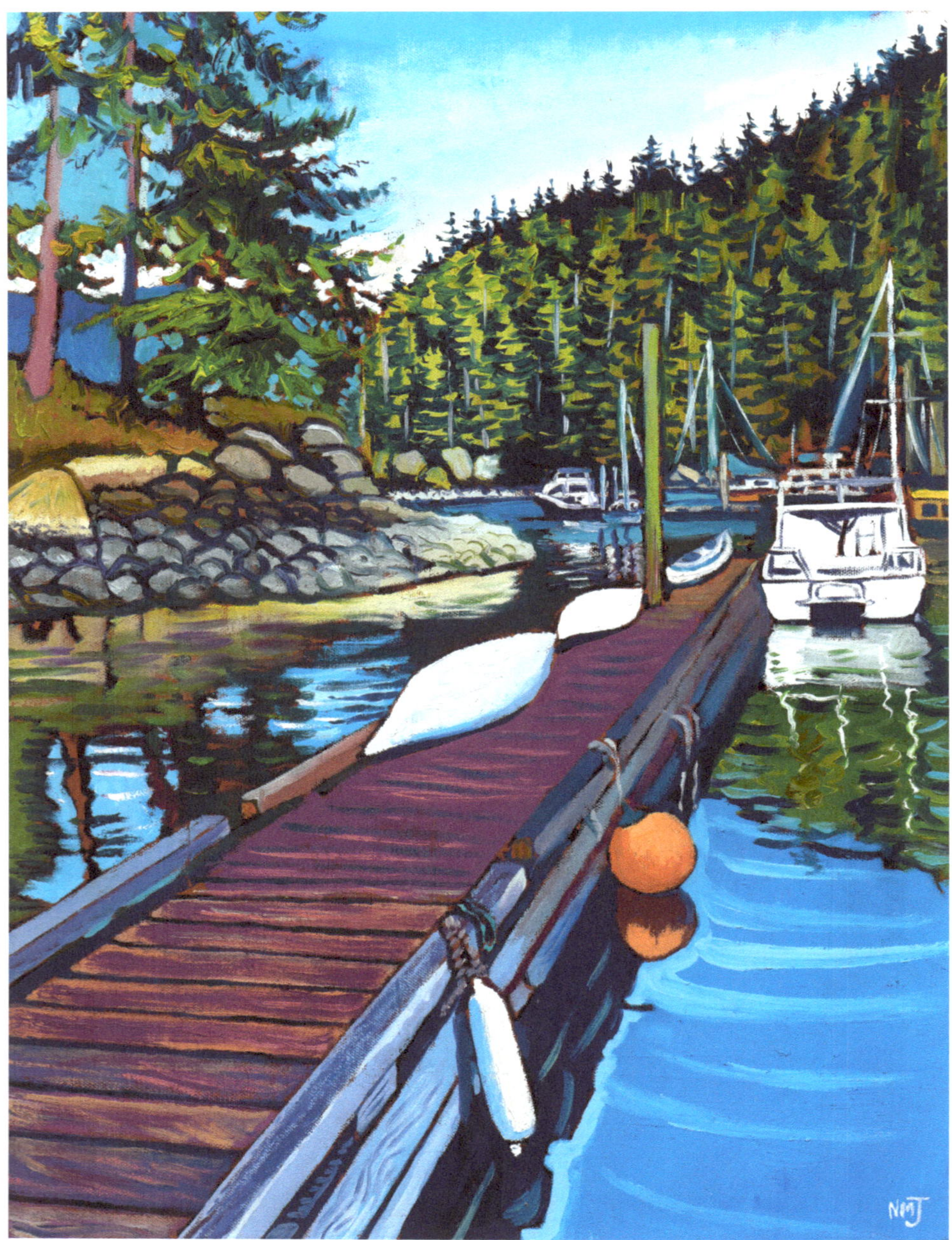

~ Bowen Island Marina, Oil. ~

Wooden wharf, above
the tide, silvered rocks
that lay far below,
a hidden tale, deep inside
the blue, a boat, a day,
and you.

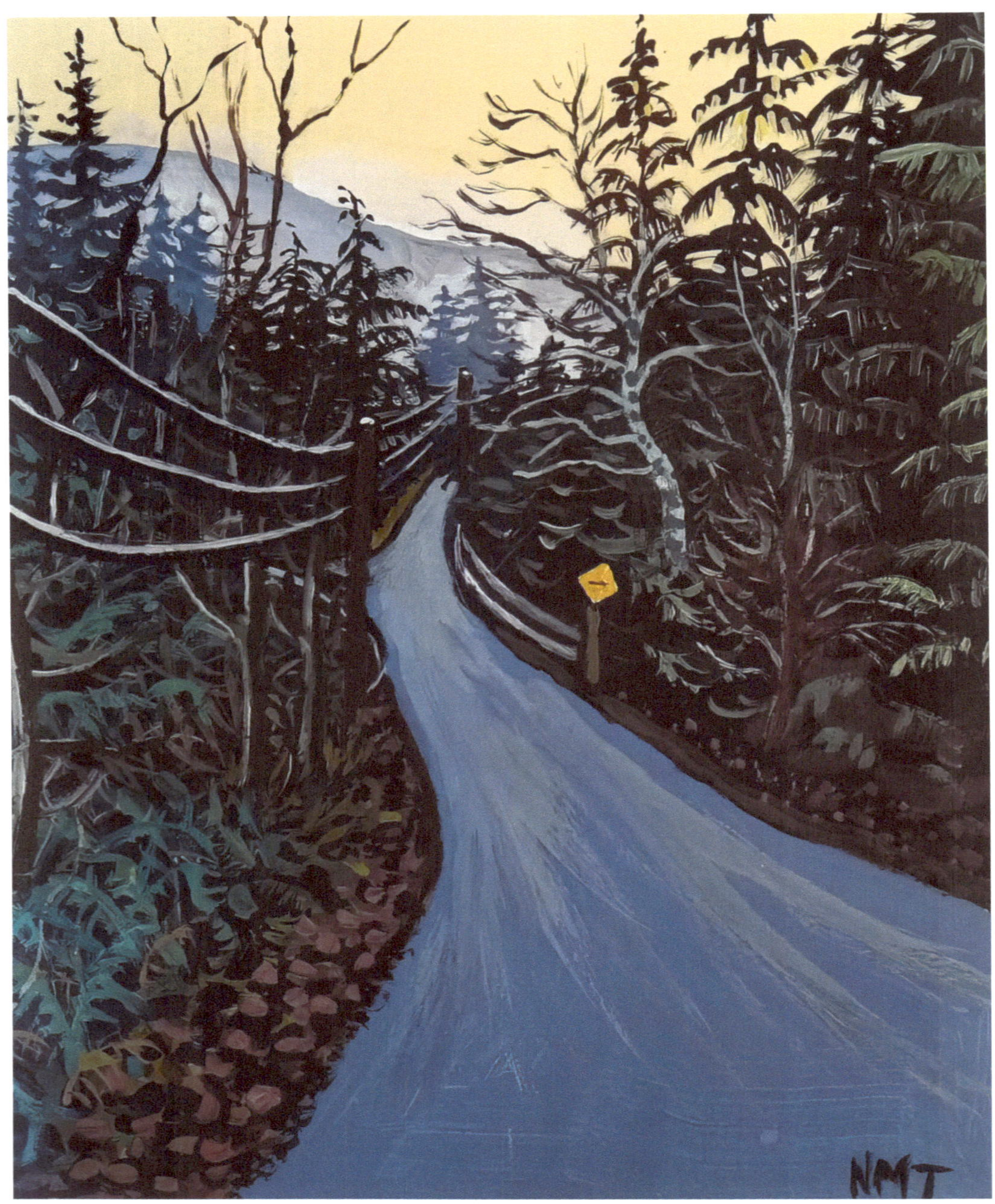

~ Fog on Mount Gardner, watercolour. ~

Ribbons in Fog

I know this island's
winding roads.
A spool of silver
mist threads tree
and sky and fence
together. There is no
yellow warning sign
that will protect us
from this scrim of fog—
it fills my eyes like ash.

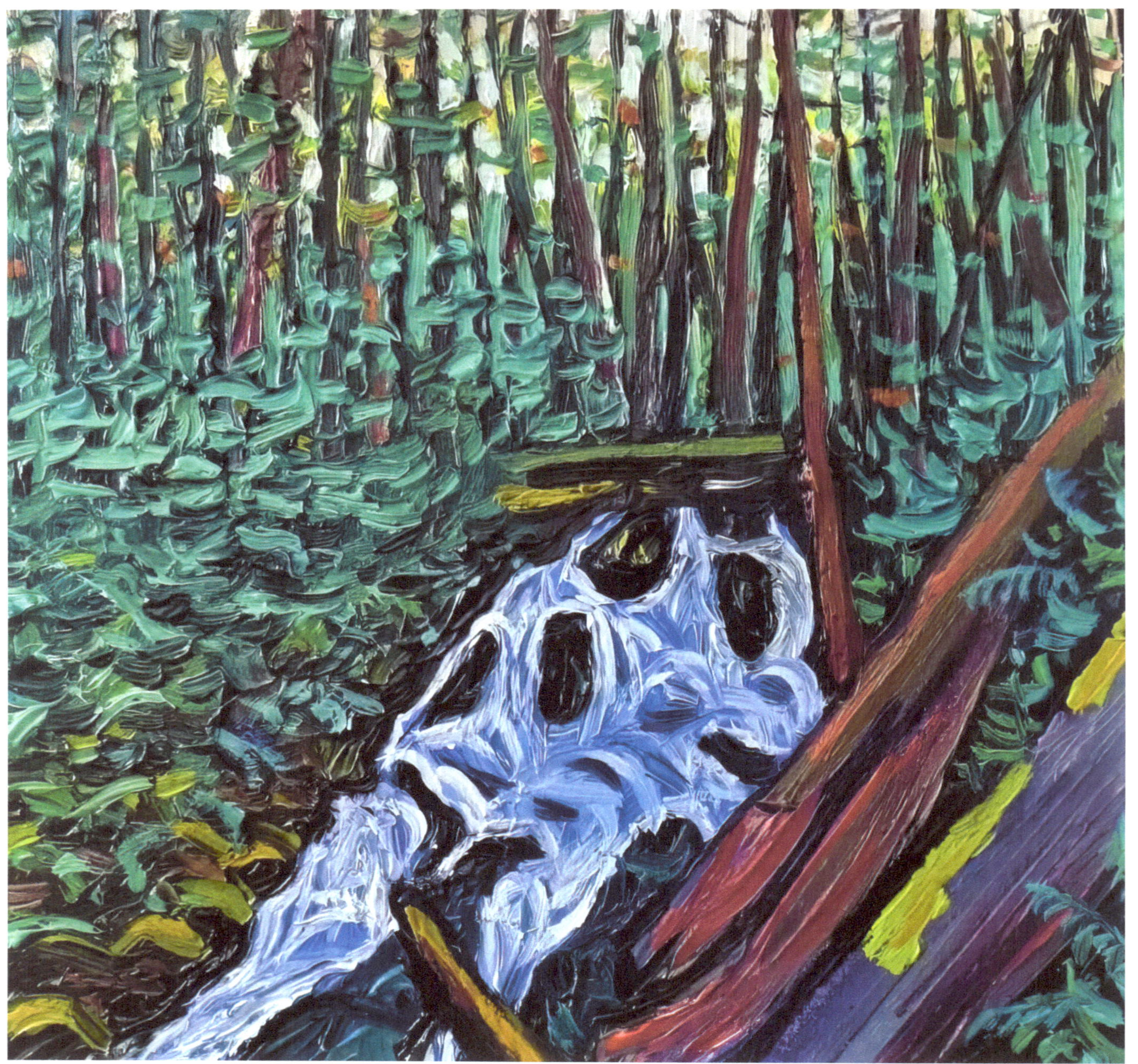

~ Waterfall on Mt. Gardner Road, oil. ~

Veil

The last thing to go
On was the veil,
Filigreed with seed pearls.
It covered the crown
Of my head and rippled
Over my shoulders.
It left no sound, but the
Gentle whisper of lace.
Like the serenity of a forest
Sewn together with the melt
And swish, of the froth
Of cool water. It spilled over
The wet ground saying,
Sanctity hides here.
The gleam of beginnings
Transforms the ordinary,
Into one altering moment—
When love surrenders easily,
To the eager hungry heart.

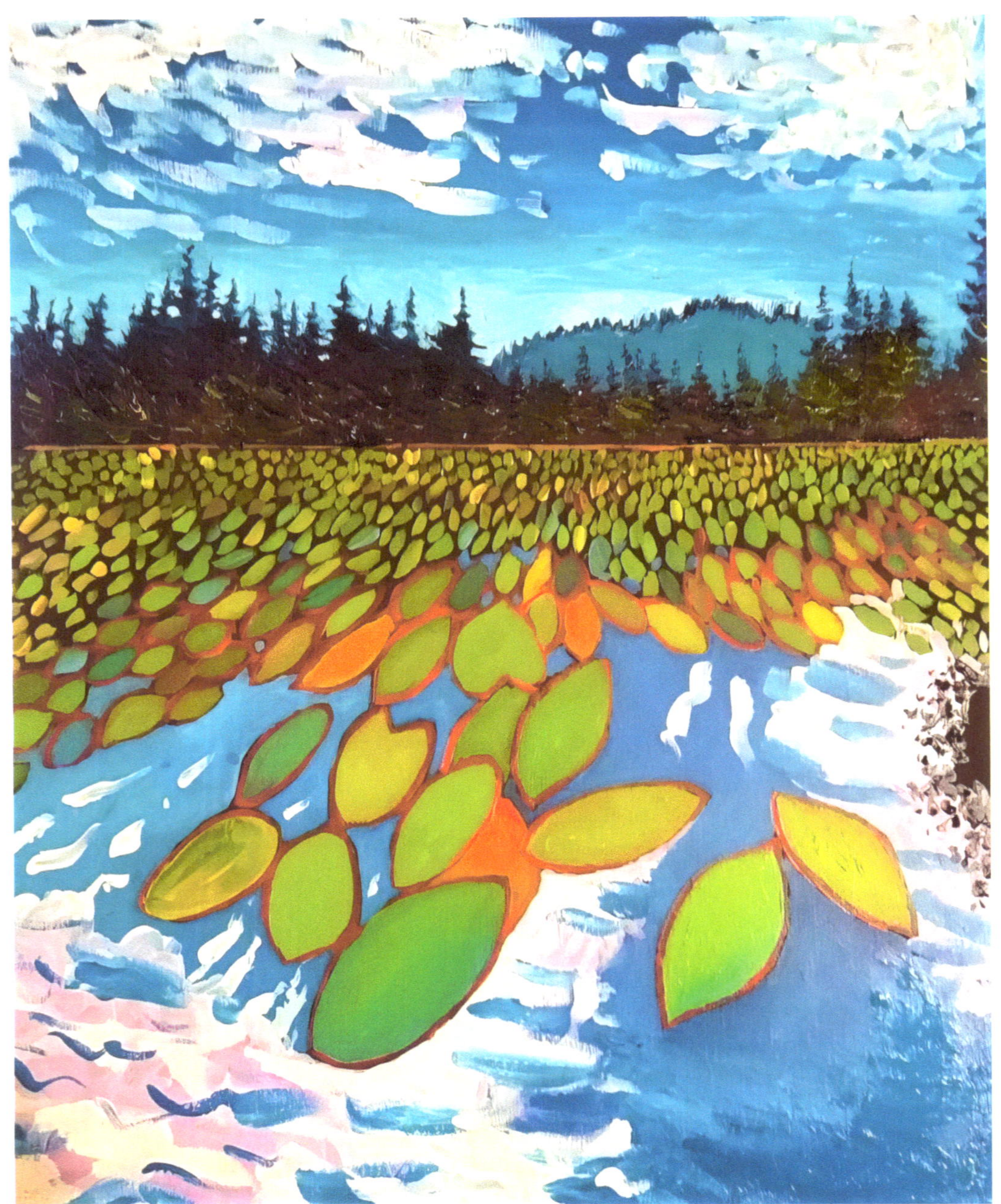

~ Killarney Lake, acrylic. ~

This lake reflects
back half my life.
She has seen me run
its circumference over
and over, when I tried to
chase guilt and make
my body disappear.
She saw me
weep when love, lost. She fed
my senses in the marshes,
with the pungent scent
of skunk cabbage.
She changed.
It snowed one fall day,
onto the ferns and moss,
framed the lake in its
autumnal abundance.
One time we built a fire,
skated on her frozen back
under a full wolf moon.
In the greening of spring,
fiddlehead ferns
lined the path
with their tenderness.

I rejoiced.
I think of summers when
my paddles held dragonflies
and our canoe floated
aimlessly, through
a confabulation of lilies.
I knew the roots and hills,
the deer trails and mud,
the grassy lookout at the top.
I leaned my back against
a stump, opened my throat
to sing—

white doves flew out.

They encircled the lake ~

like pearls.

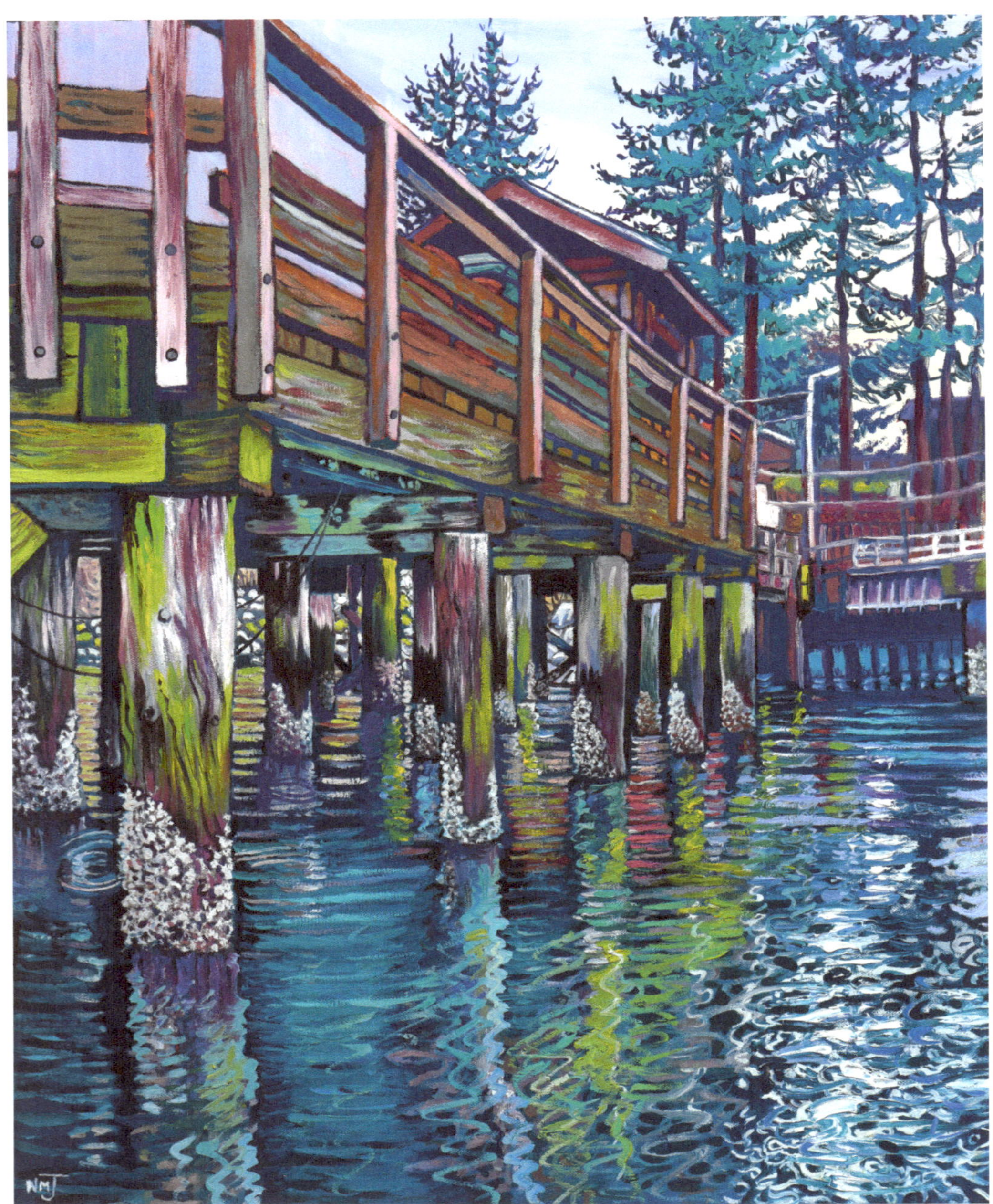

~ Snug Cove dock, oil. ~

If I was a gull, I would
land right here—tucked
into the algaed wharf,
and watch the ferry
slide into the dock.
I'd listen to the girl,
who saw me
out of her window,
when she called me
beautiful.
She'd noticed
my red tipped beak,
snowy breast,
and wings that were
edged with pewter.
I would watch
for fish swimming
in the jade waters
below.
I'd glimpse my reflection,
and see a thousand
fractured ways of flight.

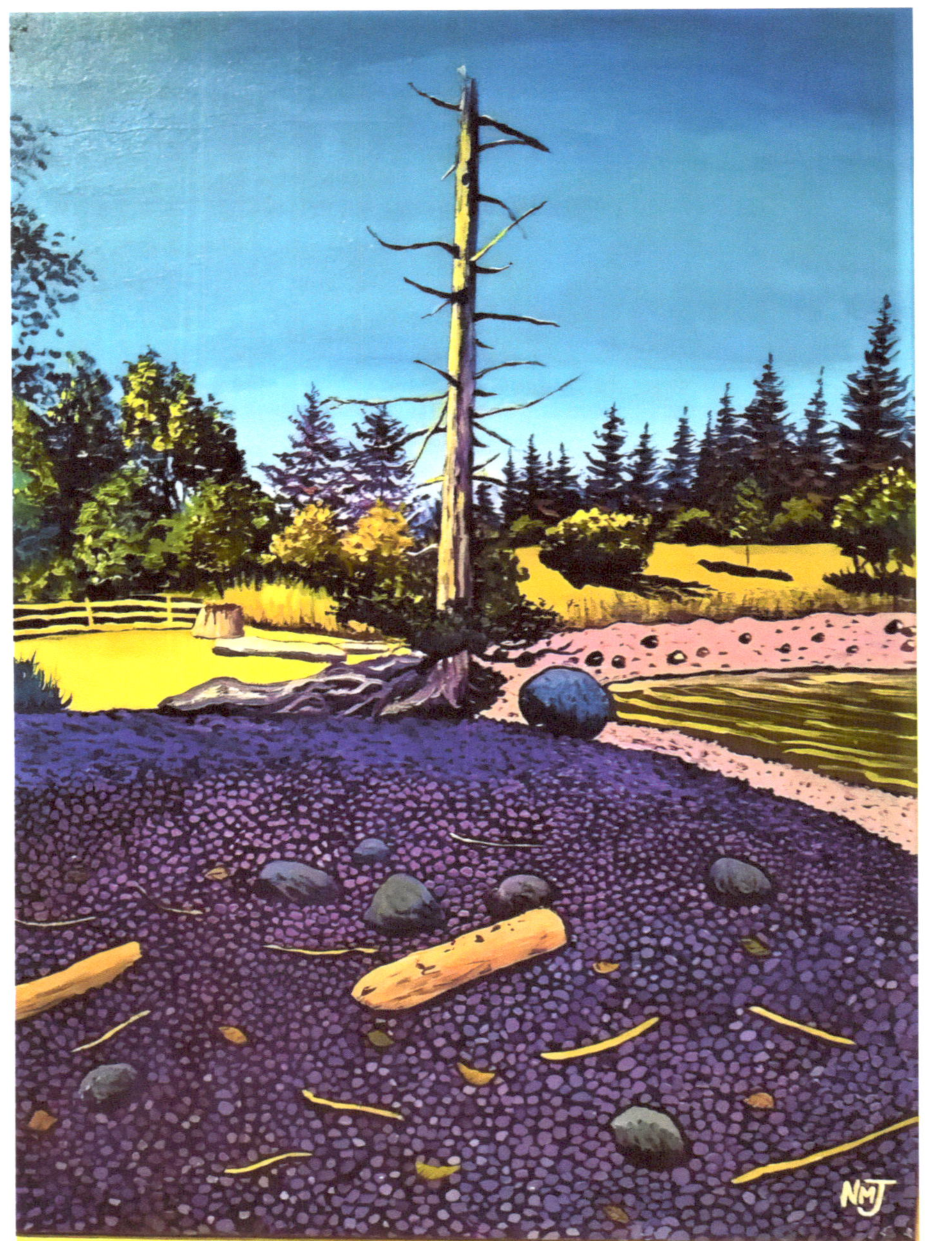

~ Tree at Snug Cove, acrylic. ~

THE TREE

This tree reminds me
of a silvered talking stick,
or King Arthur's sword
buried deep within
the stone. Oh, ancient relic,
you have so many
stories to tell—of the geese
that wander on the emerald pallet. And the dogs.
Always black and smiling, chasing and charging
through the clutch of birds.
Tails wagging as each goose
slips noisily back
into their ocean refuge.
The grass is where I spread
my blanket to feast with my family,
on bread and cheese, blackberries—
as large as my thumb.
This place remembers
the laughter of our children,
so many generations past.
They dug holes in the pebbles
looking out for crabs, too.
This lustre of a blue blue day covers me when I rest.
I count the cricket's calls,
where time is not linear.
They have been speaking
to us for centuries,
marking the years.

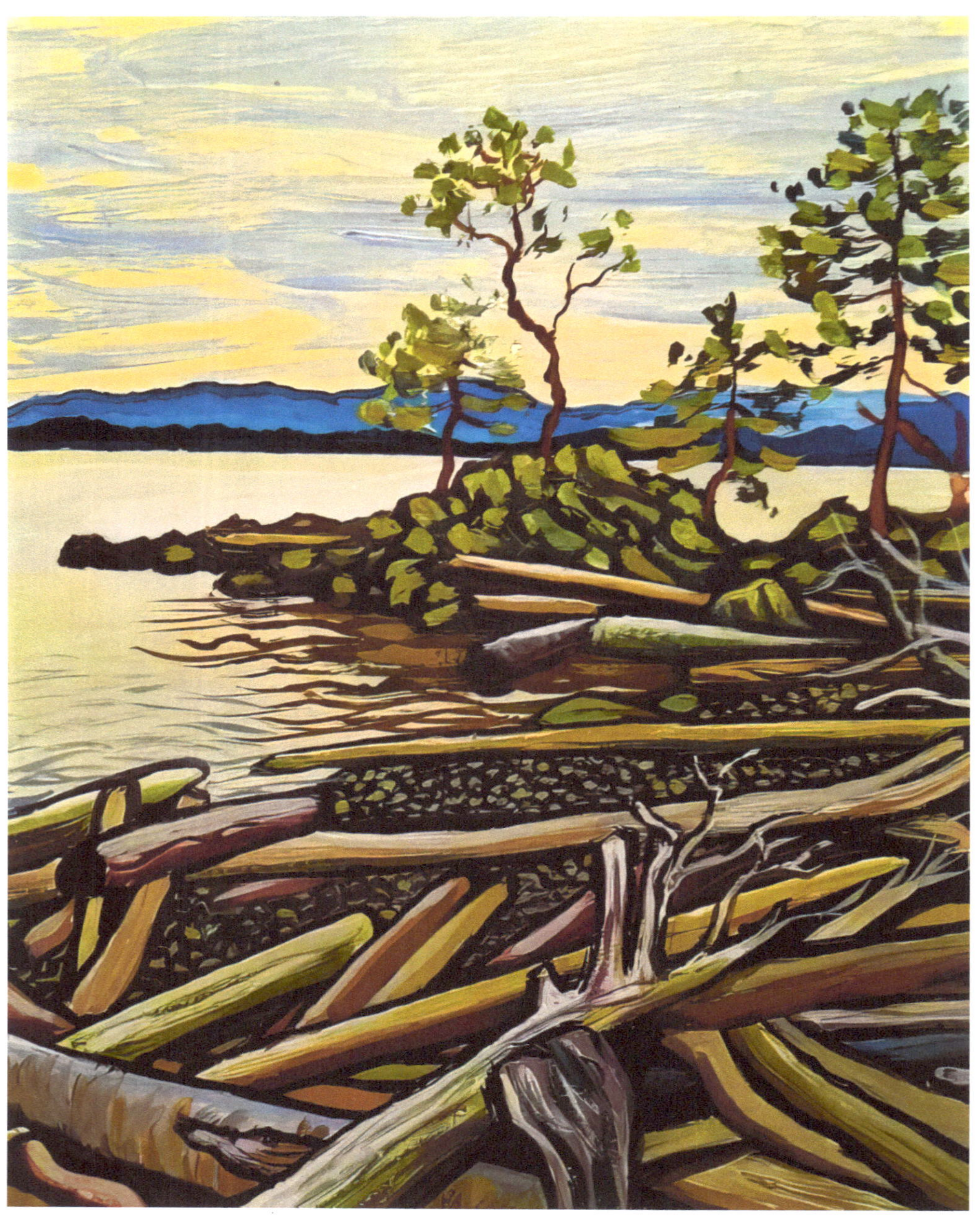

~ Arbutus Bluffs at Cape Roger Curtis, watercolour. ~

three arbutus trees grow
tangled in a mossy outcrop
their arms lift in the breeze
hailing the sky and calling it
beautiful in its feathery brush
of blue and weightless white

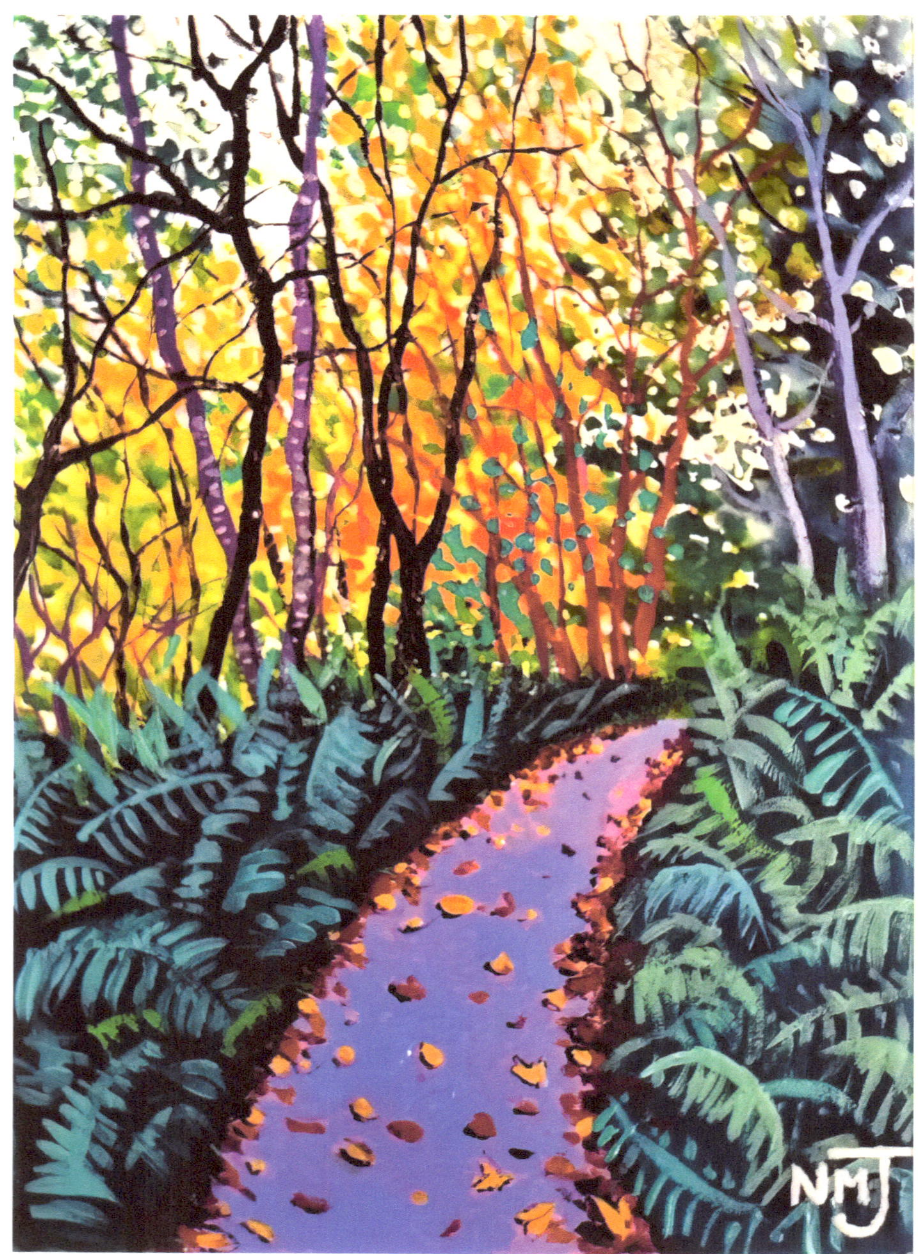

~ Alder Grove Trail, watercolour. ~

Amber and Gold

In the alder forest, frangible leaves
brush lightly against each other.
The path meanders
just ahead of me.
A lone thrushes' call echoes,
again, and then again,
as it skims over the ferns,
and into the cathedral
of saffron—in this season
of second chances.

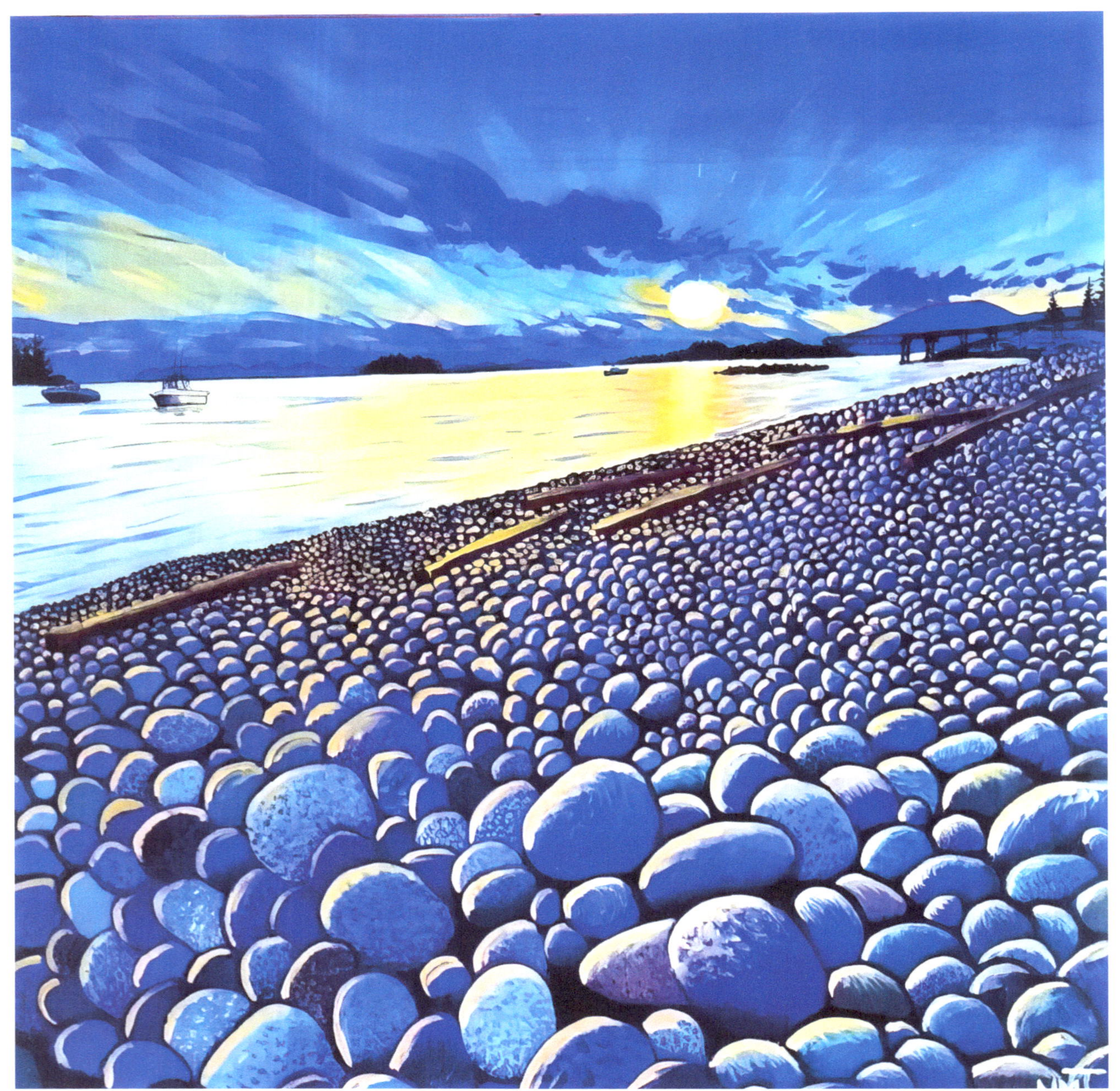

~ Tunstall Bay at Sunset, acrylic. ~

Skipping

When you were five,
you'd skip flat rocks,
and flick them
expertly, into
the mirrored sea.
They left behind
widening concentric
circles—
much like a reflection
of our own lives.
You knew how to throw
and release, a mother's
greatest quest, the picking
up and letting go, a truth
so hard for me to learn.
You once said,
'just graze the surface'.
When I did,
the stone skipped
three, four, five times,
across the sheet of gold.
You took my breath away.
For you were already
reaching towards
your future, with the flick
of a wrist, you were grown.

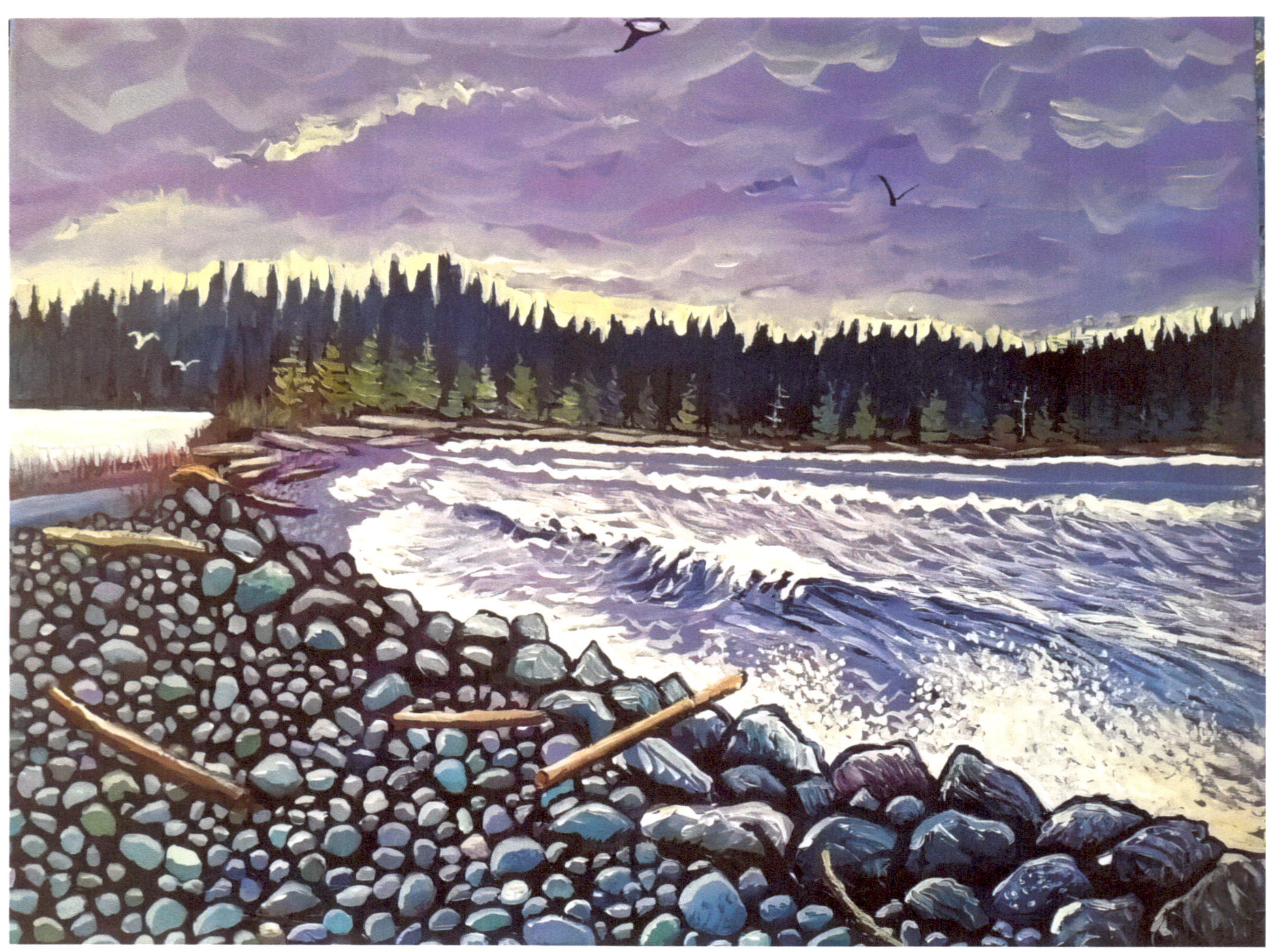

~ Whiffin Spit, Sooke, acrylic. ~

RIPTIDE

the suck of tides pulls
slick rocks and silvered froth clawing back millennia
leaves branches like Gretel's bread tossed on briney beads
of cool afternoon light

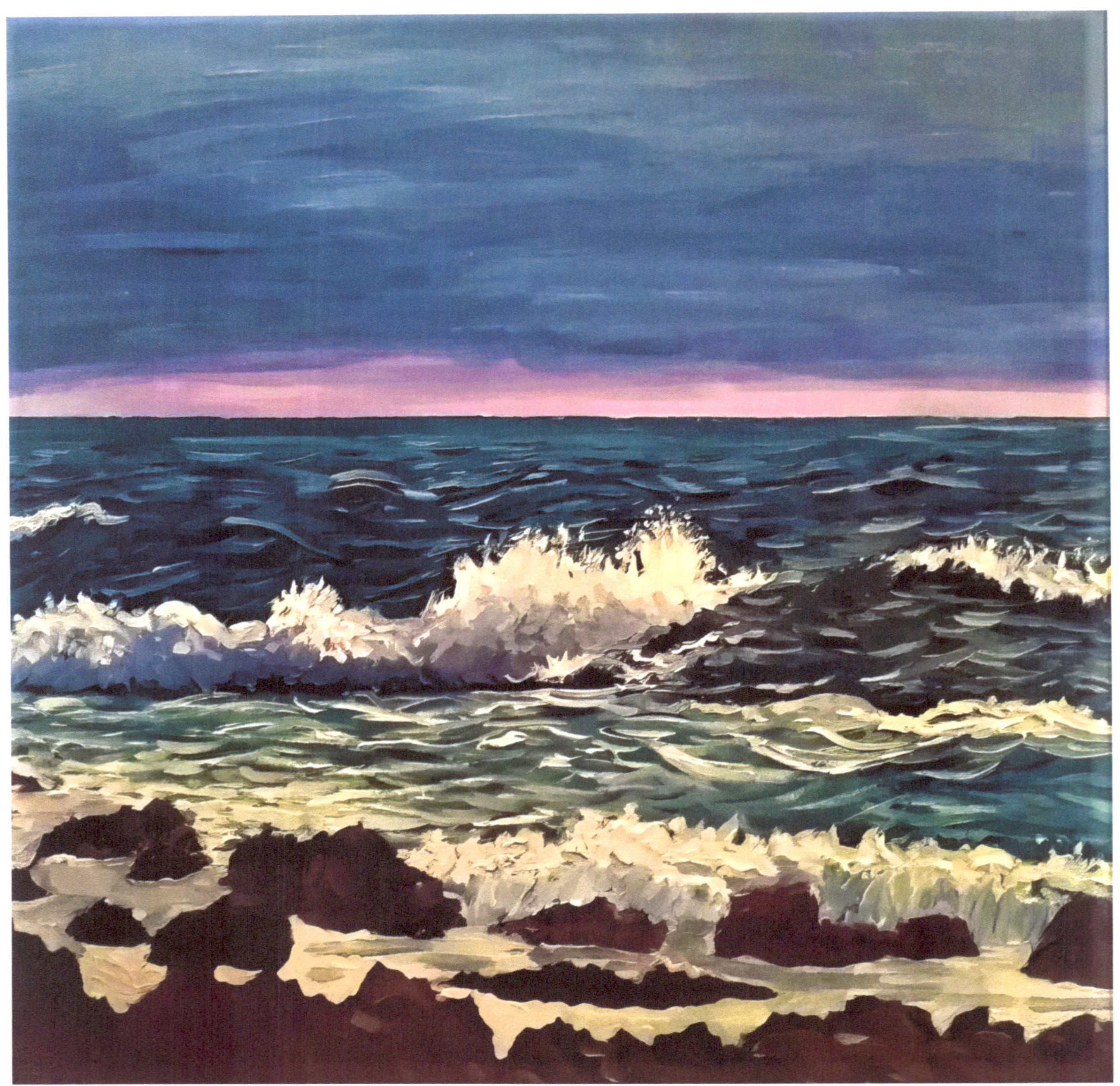

~ Tunstall Bay, oil. ~

Tempestuous
To Katie

I remember 35 years ago when the ocean froze—
making waves like wax.
They turned hard and green.
The cage of my chest,
drew in air white with salt.
This stinging
made my cheeks bloom,
even as I huddled
under down and wool.
The trees bent forward,
and laboured, clenching
black earth with their roots.
Bottle-green sea clawed
at the icy stones.
I was alive. Shouting
your name.
Singing Puccini, and spinning
in circles with you. We were
pressed
together by the surge
of the gale,
but
we weren't afraid.
I held you tightly, in awe,
at the miracle of being
together,
in this bone-chilling
Arctic storm.

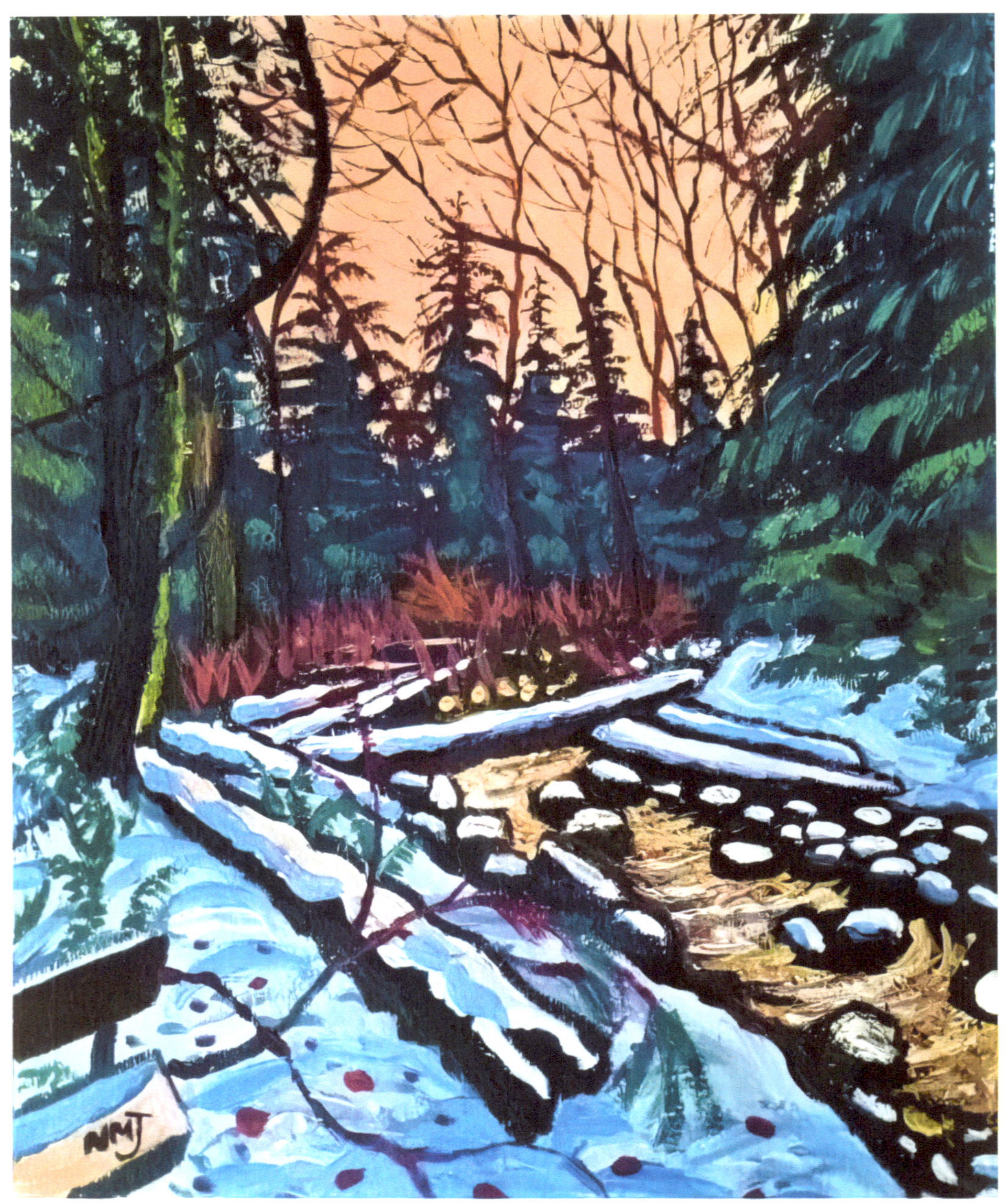

~ Creek on Mike's Lorg Trail, watercolour. ~

heavy white Russian hatted stones
lead the way to the cold path
in a forest still dipped in snow in the haze of winter with apricot skies peeking through the
sentry of trees and maroon bushes waiting for the busy chatter of remembered glory
in spring's magnificent greening

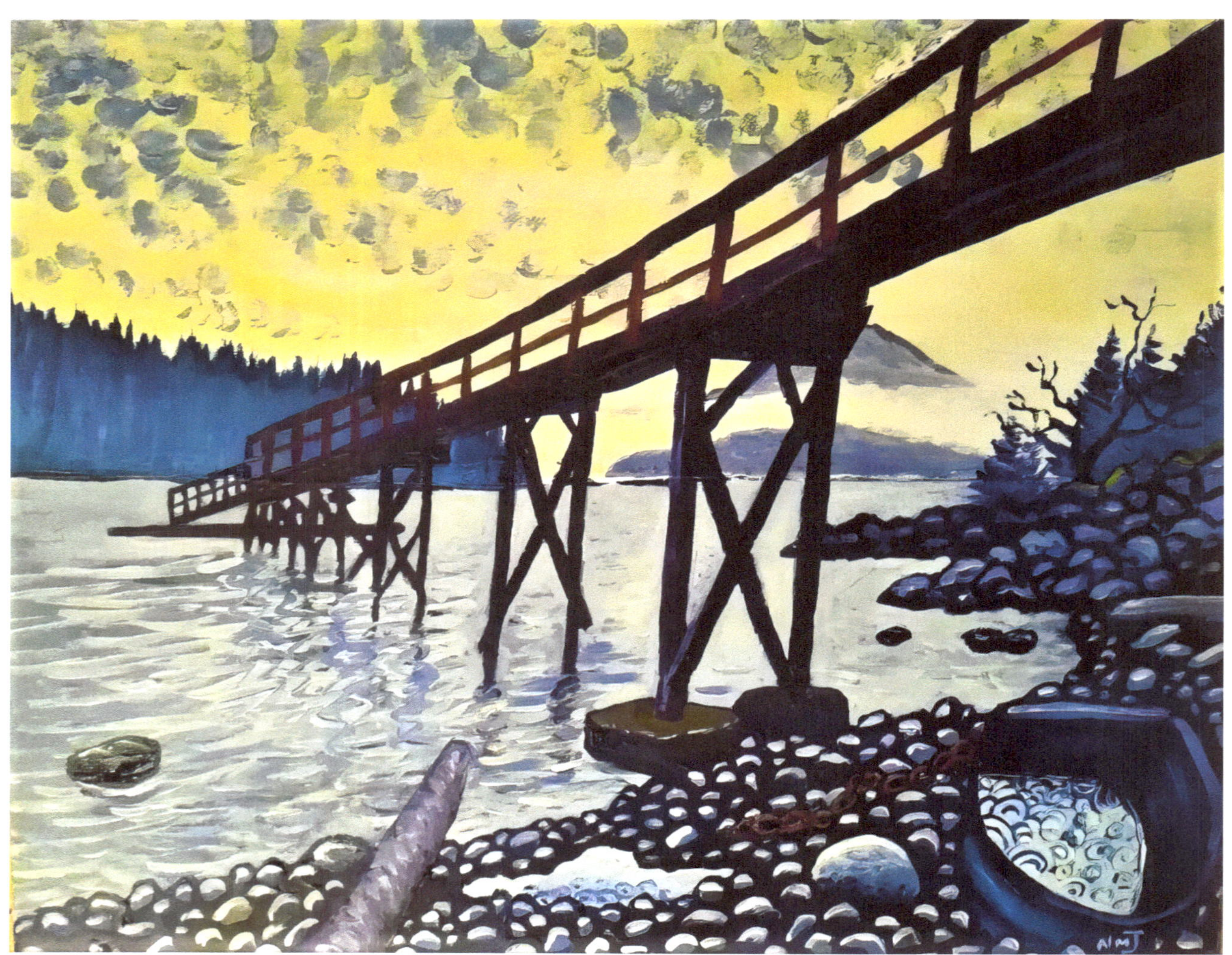

~ Mt. Gardner Dock, acrylic. ~

Our Place

My child holds my hand,
as we walk barefoot,
down the warm planked
dock. The red handrail
is a celebration, a crimson
streak on a hummingbird's cheek.
I showed you the clouds.
They looked like scales
shimmering on a salmon's
iridescent back. My little one,
here is our place.
This rock and forest and vast
pewter ocean. It laps gently
against these blue musselled footings.
Your delight as I bend to tell you a secret,
as small as
a periwinkle.
My heart is the home
you'll return to—
when dusk comes,
and daylight drains
the sky.

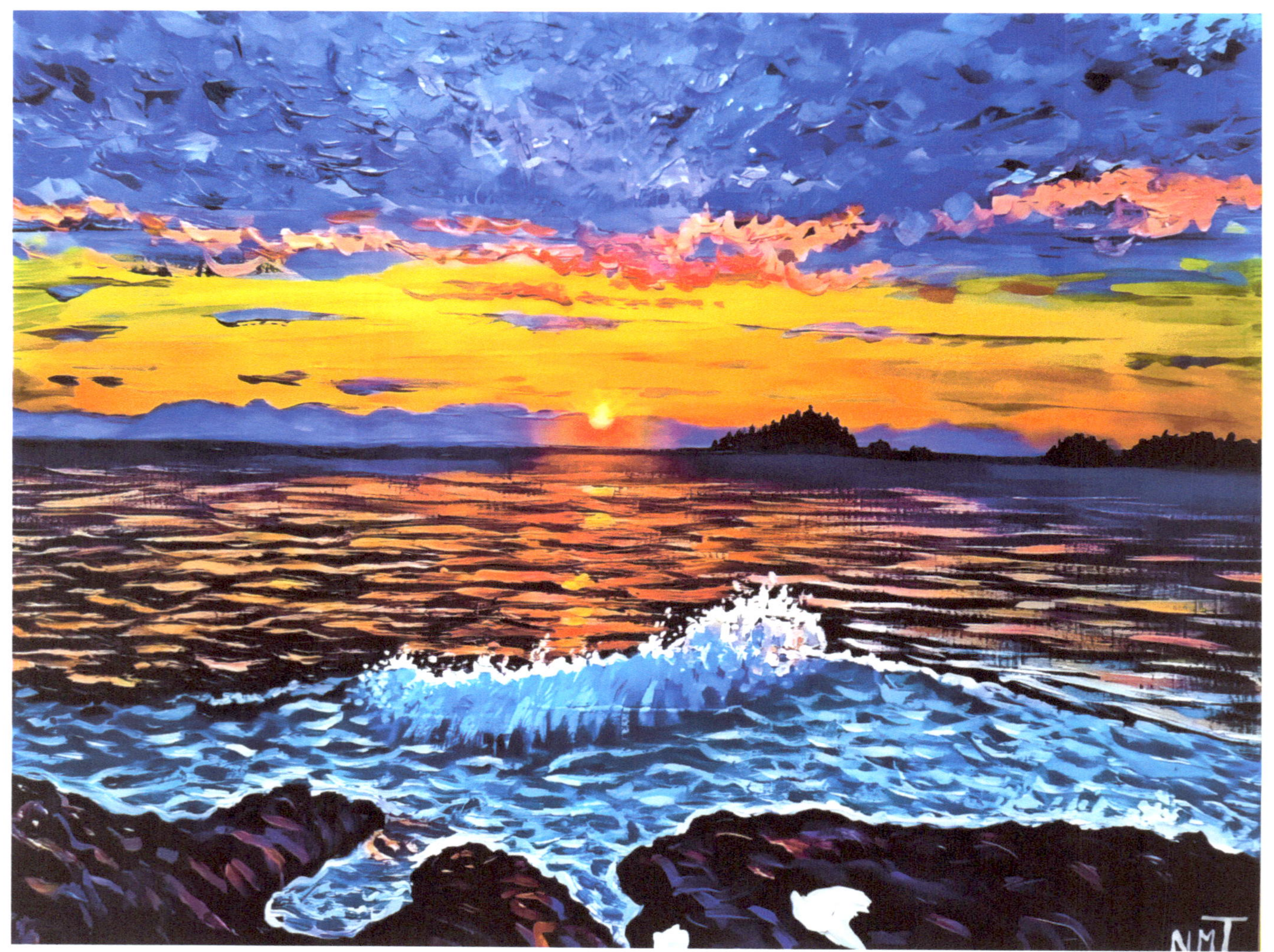

~ Collingwood Point, watercolour. ~

Glorious hues of sunset
paint the western sky.
A panoply of indigo,
russet, tangerine, stains
the Salish Sea. The orb
of day descends to its rest,
a mere golden speck
on the edge of the world.
The surf presses forward,
leaves the tracings of wind
and phosphorescent foam,
to steal across its
rock bound shore.
Then quietly,
without a sigh,
the night
comes.

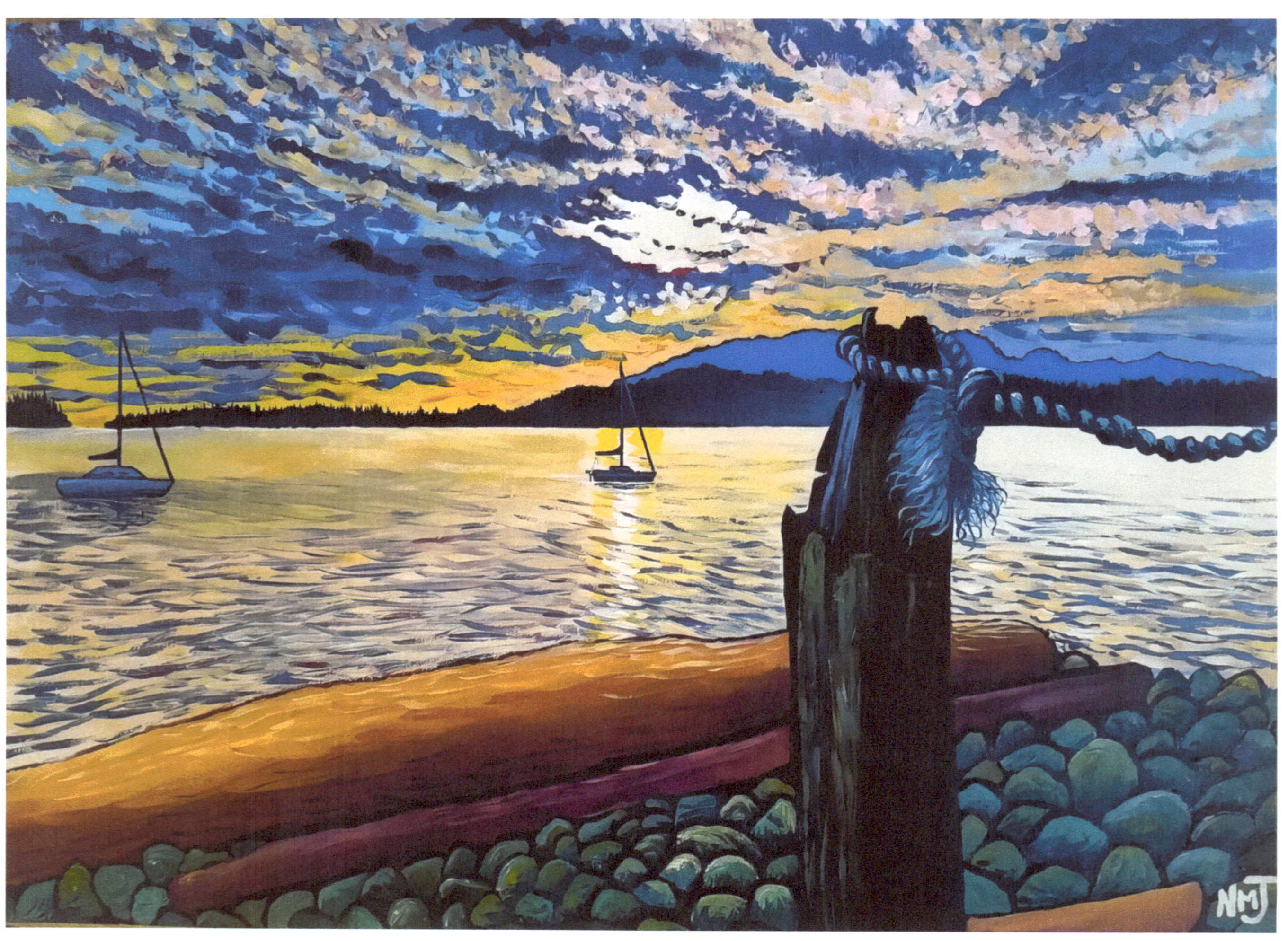

~ Sunset at Crayola Beach, acrylic. ~

TWINE AND BRINE

The boat on the left
was like my neighbour's.
I'd been in it once.
I had swallowed my fear,
long enough to stand
on the white deck.
My heart was racing
as a wave forced me
to suddenly,
awkwardly,
sit down.
No, I liked the idea of boats—
their silhouettes bobbing
in the sun on calm waters.
Indigo clouds blanket the evening.
The log I settled against
was silken, weathered.

Toward Gibsons,
were delft mountains.
They gathered this pallet
of colour to their breasts—
like stray lambs.
Picture this. Just this.
Two small boats. Braided
rope and the sky breaking
overhead. Sunset spilling like
gold onto our upturned faces.

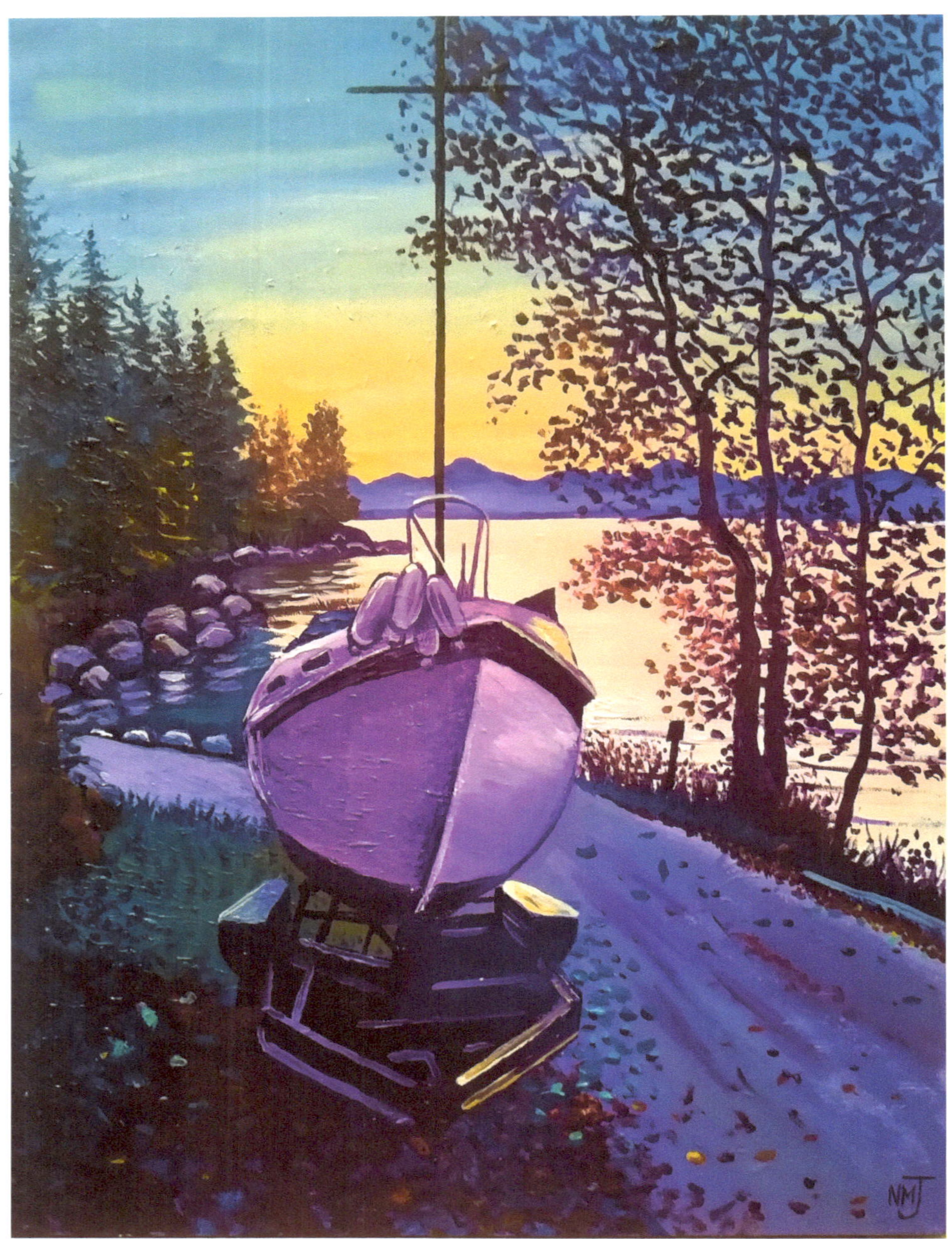

~ Tunstall Bay, acrylic. ~

Wednesday Afterglow

I watch the sunset
dip below the ridge
in all seasons. I'm always trying
to catch the last moment,
before the end
of day, the beginning
of pearly dusk. It is here
I breathed in the briney
seaweed, the sudden
offshore wind, the pungent scent
of lands, peaked
in an aurora of snow.
I fill myself with the seagulls' call,
the bell sounds,
of children laughing
as they chase the play
of waves.
Each one is a sleepy silhouette
to be carried forever,
in the comfort
of their parents'
outstretched arms.

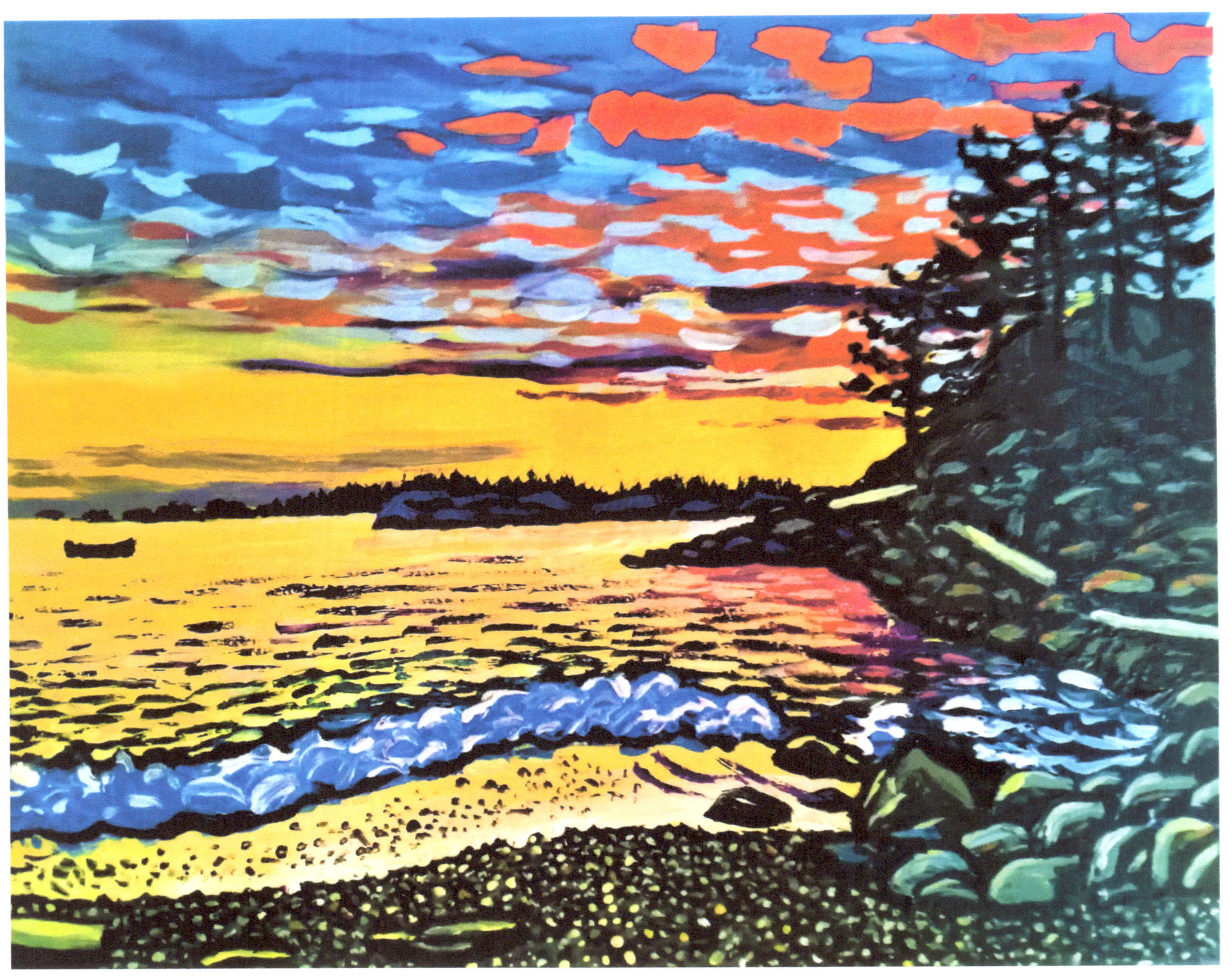

~ Cape Roger Curtis Sunset, watercolour. ~

I sit here holy, baptized
by extravagant colour,
as the day closes and
the beach has deepened
to darkness. Pebbles will be
gathered in a drawstring purse.
The melon sky hides
under clouds that change
from coral to indigo.
Being here, right here,
is a blessing
for my restless mind. Hues
of a summer evening moves
silently through the trees,
stealing their green.
Tonight's pull and push
of tides will fashion
a black womb that will
rock us all to sleep.

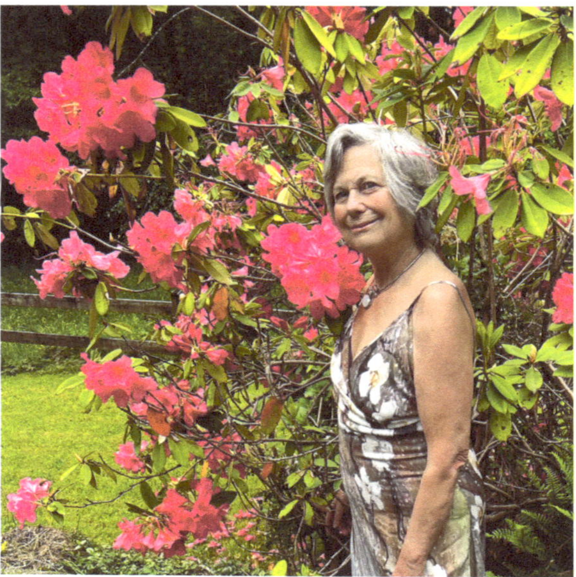

Jude Neale is a Canadian poet, vocalist, spoken word performer, and Master Educator with over 50 years of experience. She has published 11 books of poetry, and was a finalist for the Pat Lowther Memorial Award. Jude has collaborated with musicians, dancers, artists, film makers, and fellow poets. She is currently working with Nicholas Jennings, Jane Kenyon and David Woodfall in three separate projects. Her vocal and poetry CDs will be released in 2023. This volume, *Water Forgets Its Own Name*, is Jude's twelfth book.

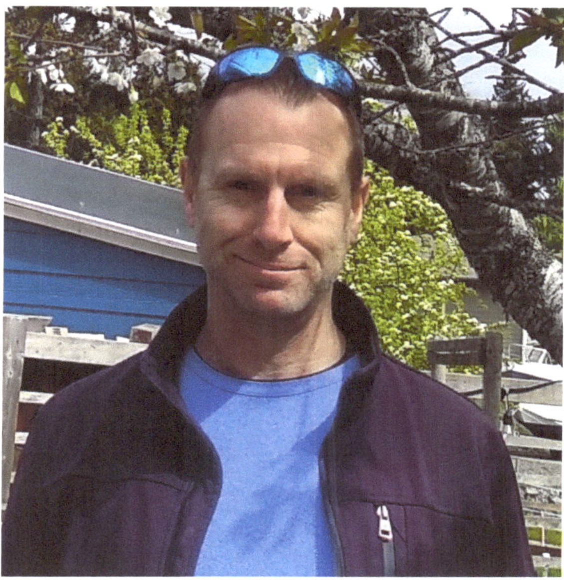

Nicholas Jennings is a prolific Bowen Island visual artist. He works with oils, gouache and acryl-ics, and has painted watercolour scenes in Portugal, Russia, Slovenia, New Zealand, Ireland, England, Mexico, and multiple locations around BC. Nick moved to Canada from the UK in 2005 to be closer to his father, who had recently retired from SFU after 50 years in the Philosophy department. He particularly enjoys exploring the textures and values created by inclement weather, as well as the richness of sunsets reflected in water, making Bowen Island the ideal place to be an artist! Nick has recently adopted the use of oils as his primary medium, but continues to paint in watercolour, using a technique he personally developed, which subverts conventional approaches. By profession, he is a lecturer specializing in academic preparation at Capilano University, and he has a master's degree in applied Linguistics from the University of Birmingham. Nick had private lessons at age nine with a celebrated local artist, later studying art, literature, philosophy and education. He belongs to the Catching Stars Gallery on Bowen Island.

Printed in the USA
CPSIA information can be obtained
at www.ICGtesting.com
LVHW070146100224
771413LV00002B/43